PROPAGANDA GIRLS

PROPAGANDA GIRLS

THE SECRET WAR *of*
THE WOMEN *in* THE OSS

LISA ROGAK

ST. MARTIN'S PRESS
NEW YORK

First published in the United States by St. Martin's Press, an imprint of St. Martin's
Publishing Group

PROPAGANDA GIRLS. Copyright © 2025 by Lisa Rogak. All rights reserved. Printed in the
United States of America. For information, address St. Martin's Publishing Group,
120 Broadway, New York, NY 10271.

www.stmartins.com

Library of Congress Cataloging-in-Publication Data

Names: Rogak, Lisa, 1962– author.
Title: Propaganda girls : the secret war of the women in the OSS / Lisa Rogak.
Other titles: Secret war of the women in the OSS
Description: First edition. | New York : St. Martin's Press, 2025. | Includes
    bibliographical references and index.
Identifiers: LCCN 2024044409 | ISBN 9781250275592 (hardcover) |
    ISBN 9781250275608 (ebook)
Subjects: LCSH: World War, 1939-1945—Propaganda. | Black
    propaganda—United States—History—20th century. | United States.
    Office of Strategic Services. Morale Operations Branch. | World War,
    1939-1945—Secret service—United States. | World War,
    1939-1945—Participation, Female. | MacDonald, Elizabeth, 1915-2015. |
    Podoski, Barbara Lee, 1914-2009 | Smith-Hutton, Jane, 1912-2002. |
    Dietrich, Marlene. | World War, 1939-1945—Women—Biography.
Classification: LCC D810.P7 U476 2025 | DDC 940.54/86730922—
    dc23/eng/20241002
LC record available at https://lccn.loc.gov/2024044409

Our books may be purchased in bulk for promotional, educational, or business
use. Please contact your local bookseller or the Macmillan Corporate and
Premium Sales Department at 1-800-221-7945, extension 5442, or by email at
MacmillanSpecialMarkets@macmillan.com.

First Edition: 2025

10 9 8 7 6 5 4 3 2 1

For Alex

CONTENTS

Introduction   1

ACT ONE: GOING TO WAR

Chapter 1. Betty   9

Chapter 2. Zuzka   24

Chapter 3. Jane   34

Chapter 4. Marlene   49

ACT TWO: GLORIOUS AMATEURS

Chapter 5. Zuzka   63

Chapter 6. Betty   77

Chapter 7. Marlene   91

Chapter 8. Jane   103

ACT THREE: BELIEVABLE LIES

Chapter 9. Zuzka   117

Chapter 10. Marlene   132

Chapter 11. Jane   144

Chapter 12. Betty   156

ACT FOUR: BACK TO REALITY

Chapter 13. Zuzka   169

Chapter 14. Marlene   178

Chapter 15. Betty   185

Chapter 16. Jane   191

Acknowledgments   197

Notes   199

Bibliography   212

Index   217

PROPAGANDA
GIRLS

Introduction

During the last brutal eighteen months of World War II, American troops in the European and Far East theaters began to notice a significant uptick in the number of Axis soldiers and collaborators who were surrendering—peacefully and willingly—to the Allies.

Defeated German and Japanese troops stumbled across enemy lines in Europe and Asia with one hand thrust in the air, waving a piece of paper with the other. In some cases, it was a tattered scrap of fabric fashioned into the globally recognized white flag of surrender. But many of the war-weary soldiers brandished leaflets, newspapers, and letters that had served as their personal breaking points, convincing them that theirs was a war that was no longer worth fighting for. One half-starved German even handed over a couple sheets of rough toilet paper with Hitler's face printed on it as his ticket out of the war.

The Allied welcoming committee patted down the enemy soldiers before sending them on to intelligence officers, followed by the first good meal they'd had in months. They tossed the well-creased, sweat-stained papers in the burn pile along with their enemies' threadbare uniforms.

Neither the Allied nor Axis soldiers realized it, but many of the broadsides, pamphlets, and other documents the defectors presented in surrender came from a common source. What's more, they were totally fake, a secret brand of propaganda produced by a small group of women who spent the last years of the war conjuring up lies, stories, and rumors with the sole aim to break the morale of Axis soldiers. These women worked in the European theater, across enemy lines in occupied China, and in Washington, DC, and together and separately, they forged letters and "official" military orders, wrote and produced entire newspapers, scripted radio broadcasts and songs, and even developed rumors for undercover spies and double agents to spread to the enemy.

Outside of a small group of spies, no one knew they existed.

* * *

The four women of *Propaganda Girls*—Elizabeth "Betty" MacDonald, Jane Smith-Hutton, Barbara "Zuzka" Lauwers, and celebrated German-American actress Marlene Dietrich—worked for General "Wild Bill" Donovan's Office of Strategic Services, or OSS, the precursor of today's CIA. Their department, the Morale Operations branch—or MO—was in charge of producing "black propaganda," defined as any leaflet, poster, radio broadcast, or other public or private media that appeared to come from *within* the enemy country, either from a resistance movement or from disgruntled soldiers and civilians. In essence, black propaganda was a series of believable lies designed to cause the enemy soldiers to lose heart and ultimately surrender, but it was also aimed at occupied populations and soldiers captured for cheap labor, to encourage them to rise up against their oppressors and join the winning side.

Donovan, who had studied Nazi black propaganda, knew how effective these tactics could be. "Subtly planned rumor and propaganda [can] subvert people from allegiance to their own country," he said. "It is essentially a weapon of exploitation, and if successful can be more effective than a shooting war." While officers in other departments refused to hire women, Donovan specifically searched them out when he began to staff his new MO branch, as he believed they would excel at creating subversive materials.

"General Donovan believed that we could do things that the men couldn't," Betty said years later. "We were able to think of a lot of gossipy things to do for MO that men never would have thought of. I don't want to brag, but women can hurt people better, maybe, than men could think of. Women seemed to have a feeling for how to really fool people."

*   *   *

Donovan liked quirky people, and Betty, Zuzka, Jane, and Marlene definitely fit the bill. All had careers that were highly unusual for women in the 1930s and '40s, and they all yearned to escape the gender restrictions of the day that dictated they be mothers and wives, or teachers or nurses if they absolutely *had* to work. They all wanted more than their present lives provided, though they never lost sight of the fact that their efforts would have just one aim: to help win the war and bring American soldiers back home.

Their motivations for joining the OSS differed—two wanted vengeance, two craved adventure—and one served stateside while three headed overseas. But the one thing they shared in common was that all four were determined to serve their country in the best way they could: by using their brains.

Every office and project in every theater was woefully understaffed, so the women quickly learned to multitask everything while happily taking advantage of the utter lack of supervision to call their own shots. While the women often turned to spies and agents for intel to help them craft their writings, they occasionally had to do the dirty work themselves.

And because the work was so clandestine, when it came to paying contract workers and locals for their assignments, a little bit of creativity was in order: Betty became well practiced at slicing off the exact amount of opium to compensate a Burmese spy, while Zuzka paid a group of German POWs with an afternoon at a local Italian brothel.

The four women loved their jobs along with the autonomy they brought, while at the same time faced a boatload of challenges regardless of where they were serving. The women had to constantly fight for promotions and recognition, as well as deal with rampant sexism. Often, after her workday was done, Betty was called upon to serve coffee and sandwiches to her male coworkers, while Zuzka played cocktail waitress, serving drinks to male officers who she had brainstormed alongside just minutes before. But they took it in stride. As Zuzka put it, "*Scheuklappen*, we were always reminded, German for blinders," she said. "Just look straight ahead at what you're doing, and don't worry about what the other guys are doing."

The stakes were high: They knew that not every "believable lie" they made up worked out, and there was the hard truth that people died as a result of their brainstorms. "I tried to push it out of my head," said Betty.

The women also faced constant danger, and their own lives were often at risk: Betty worked in India and behind enemy lines in China, where a sizable contingent of locals didn't want the Americans interfering in their affairs. Zuzka regularly interrogated German POWs who could snuff out her life with one well-aimed finger to the throat. And Hitler had placed a bounty on Marlene's capture from the moment she became a US citizen.

But if one more leaflet, radio broadcast, or well-turned phrase would cause just one German soldier to feel that maybe Hitler wasn't worth fighting for any longer, well then it was worth the twelve-hour days, giant bugs, lousy food, and living in tents thousands of miles from home.

The women were extremely productive over the roughly eighteen months they worked for the OSS, cranking out hundreds of articles, letters, leaflets, and radio scripts. They even intercepted postcards and letters from enemy soldiers, erasing any positive messages and instead adding news of starvation and lost battles to dishearten family back home. The women had to take particular care to make sure each piece would "pass," that civilians and troops would believe it came from a resister or disgruntled soldier from within their own country. If there were any doubts, Allied soldiers could be at risk.

* * *

When the women who would become known as Donovan's Dreamers first came on board, Donovan gave them some plum advice, words that none of the women had heard before:

"If you think it will work, go ahead."

For these unconventional women, planting victory gardens, wrapping bandages, and buying war bonds wasn't going to cut it. Wild Bill was happy to help. He needed highly intelligent and creative women who could think on their feet, were fluent in at least one foreign language, and could hit the ground running.

In Betty MacDonald (later McIntosh), Barbara "Zuzka" Lauwers, Jane Smith-Hutton, and Marlene Dietrich, he had found four of the best.

ACT ONE

GOING
TO WAR

Chapter 1

Betty

For Elizabeth "Betty" MacDonald, the morning of Sunday, December 7, 1941, dawned like most days on the island of Oahu: sheer paradise. Warm and sunny with a light westerly breeze passing through the windows of the home in the mountains in Koko Head that she shared with her husband, Alex. The couple's small, neat house overlooked a lagoon, and was just ten miles away from downtown, where they both worked as newspaper reporters.

Betty loved her job as society and women's editor at the *Honolulu Star-Bulletin*, but her beat presented her with a nonstop soft-news cycle of luncheons, parades, and church fairs. At dinner each night, she listened to Alex's tales of crime and corruption as a police reporter at the *Honolulu Advertiser* with barely concealed envy. She yearned for stories she could sink her teeth into, and regularly pestered her editor to switch her to the city desk, but he always said it was no place for a woman.

To compensate for the lack of a real challenge in her day job, she threw herself into studying Asian culture. Earlier in the year, she had traveled on an army transport to the Philippines for a series of stories for the paper, and she wanted to do more. Betty and Alex had lived with a Japanese family a couple of years earlier so they could become fluent in the language and customs.

This morning, she woke just after eight o'clock and decided to let her husband sleep in; they'd been to a party the night before and Alex was a bit hungover. Betty switched on the radio to listen to the Mormon Tabernacle Choir while she waited for the coffee to percolate. Just as she was taking her first sip, a harsh buzz interrupted the mellifluous tones of the singers.

Another drill, Betty thought. Like other Oahu residents, she was long accustomed to the regular emergency alerts that were broadcast over the radio due to proximity to the naval base and Hickam Air Field at Pearl Harbor. The alerts had become so frequent that most residents tuned them out, and indeed, a couple of minutes later, the choir returned to their hymns just as Betty poured more coffee. But then the phone jangled, and she picked up after the first ring to avoid waking Alex.

"Something's happened down at Hickam," her photographer Allen "Hump" Campbell blurted out, skipping his usual pleasantries. "We need to get down to the base *now*."

News of the war in Europe and in the Pacific appeared regularly in the paper, but many citizens tuned it out. After all, the various battles and skirmishes were thousands of miles away. Besides, many residents of Hawaii—at the time a US territory, not a full-fledged state—had already lived through the destruction of World War I and had become isolationists as a result, against war at any cost.

But Betty had recently covered stories about troop movements in and out of Oahu on their way to other parts of the world, so she knew something was brewing. Even she, though, had no way to predict the enormity of what was to come.

She gulped her coffee past the lump in her throat, but in addition to fear, she had to admit that she felt something else: a frisson of excitement. Maybe now I'll get to cover something more than flower shows and society luncheons, she thought.

As soon as she hung up, the phone rang again. This time it was Alex's editor with the same message: Get down here *now*.

She shook her husband awake and poured him a coffee. He threw on some clothes, and after a quick kiss, he ran out the door. As a police reporter, Alex was waved through police lines and yellow-taped crime scenes, but Betty needed a male escort to gain access to anything more than the usual ladies' social events that she covered, and women were never allowed onto the military bases, escort or not. She downed the rest of her coffee while she waited for Hump to show up, and that's when she first heard it, a low rumble coming from the west. She switched off the radio and heard it again, louder this time: a boom followed by several muffled explosions.

A bomb.

Hump pulled up to the house a few minutes later, slowing down just enough for Betty to yank open the door and hop in. As they raced toward the harbor, they passed people walking their dogs and others heading to church. Palm trees lining the roads swayed in the light breeze. Just another Sunday morning on Oahu. Betty's mind started playing tricks on her. Had she imagined the explosions? Maybe it was a drill after all.

She relaxed slightly, but then she saw the birds. At first, a few small, feathered bodies peppered the sidewalk, mostly doves and sparrows. They looked peaceful, as if they were napping. A few short blocks later, tiny corpses covered the asphalt, their feathers ruffled and askew. Hump's jaw clenched as he swerved to avoid the birds, mostly unsuccessfully.

The concussion of the bombing had killed them.

This was no drill.

As their car crested the hill near the Punchbowl neighborhood, the ocean came into view. Betty never tired of the sight of Pearl Harbor and the sugarcane fields sprawled out in the distance. But now she only saw thick columns of smoke billowing up into the sky from the harbor. The water looked like it was on fire.

A few small fighter planes loop-de-looped in graceful arcs overhead. Betty craned her head outside the window. The insignia on the side of the plane was a red circle, the symbol of Japan, land of the rising sun.

"Suddenly, there was a sharp whistling sound, almost over my shoulder, and I saw a rooftop fly into the air like a pasteboard movie set," she remembered years later.

She watched as the planes turned toward the harbor, where they paused momentarily in midair before plunging straight down into the ocean.

"For the first time, I felt that numb terror that all of London has known for months, of not being able to do anything but fall on your stomach and hope the bomb won't land on you," she said. "It's the terror of sudden visions of a ripping sensation in your back, shrapnel coursing through your chest, total blackness, maybe death."

The war had finally come to America.

* * *

Betty and Hump reached King Street—then, as now, a major commercial area in the city—and ditched the car. They headed out on foot, dodging shards of broken glass, exploded bits of drywall, and shredded bamboo. They passed the drugstore where she often camped out with a Coke, trading good-natured barbs with the young soda jerk in the hopes he would pass along a juicy bit of local gossip she could use for a story.

At least she thought it was the drugstore; the walls and roof were totally gone, and tinsel and shredded holiday wrapping paper hung from the eaves.

From the time she'd jumped into Hump's car, Betty was on the automatic pilot that many reporters shift into when on the trail of a good story. She was too busy scribbling to realize that she was down to the last few sheets of her notebook. But now it hit home. Last night, she and Alex had been having fun with friends, eating and drinking too much. How did she suddenly end up in the middle of a war zone?

She glanced at the marble soda fountain counter coated with a thick layer of pale ash, a half-eaten chocolate sundae perched at the far end. At the foot of one of the stools was a stack of writing paper.

Half of the sheets were bloated, but the other half were relatively dry. She pushed the ragged pages into her pocket.

Hump gestured toward what had been the back wall of the drugstore; there was a fruit and vegetable market out back. A little boy sat cross-legged on the floor, surrounded by splintered fruit crates. Exploded pineapples and papayas revealed their flesh in a way Betty found almost obscene.

The boy was around five years old and dressed in a Buster Brown outfit and knee socks and sandals. He was smiling and humming softly as he played with a Christmas ribbon, running the end of the ribbon through one hand before repeating the process with the other. Maybe he lived nearby.

Hump took a few steps toward the boy. He and Betty traded slightly raised eyebrows, photographer-reporter shorthand for when you spot a perfect picture but don't want to spoil the mood. The kid, clearly in shock, hadn't seen them. At that moment, his whole world revolved around that ribbon.

"The kid is too happy," Hump whispered to Betty. "Can you do something about that?"

Betty and Alex didn't have children, but she felt protective of the boy. Where were his parents? Were they still alive?

She swallowed hard and knelt down beside the boy, his pudgy cheeks smudged with ash and char. She offered up a few words about the ribbon, and he looked up at her with vacant eyes. As she contemplated her next move in the name of the Fourth Estate, she automatically asked forgiveness from whatever God could allow this degree of human devastation and reached for his little arm.

Then she pinched him. *Hard.*

A moment of stunned silence was quickly pierced by the shrill wail and shocked tears of a grieving child, probably shriller than they would have been twenty-four hours earlier.

Betty jumped back and Hump moved in for his shot. When he was done, she patted the boy's head to comfort him, and she and Hump returned to navigating King Street.

A week later, Hump's photo of the sobbing boy ran in *Life* magazine.

She felt bad for the boy, but a strange and satisfying energy coursed through her veins. She had forgotten about that old reporter's trick of tweaking a source to get a good story or photo, something she rarely called upon when interviewing yet another Honolulu matron about her latest gala event. In any case, it felt good to be doing something, anything, in the wake of such unfathomable ruin.

* * *

They got back in the car and headed for the harbor. Betty's nostrils flared at the pungent smell of explosives, and the burning diesel fuel made her eyes water; the ocean *was* on fire. She stared at the bubbles percolating on the surface of the sea, rising up from the submerged ships with their men still trapped. Some alive, she thought, but not for long. Betty steeled herself—that was her job, after all—and continued to scribble on the notepaper she'd taken from the drugstore as they headed for the harbor.

The attack had been only an hour ago, but the guards at Hickam looked like they hadn't slept in days. They were able to remember, though, that women weren't allowed on the base, so they waved Hump in but not Betty. She made a quick call to her editor, who told her to head for the emergency room at Queen's Hospital instead.

"Write something from the women's point of view," he told her.

What? she thought. She was in shock, still not processing the destruction that had descended upon her beloved Oahu. But through the thickness of that terrible day, his words came through loud and clear. "I couldn't figure out why the women should be any different from the men," she said decades later.

She headed to the hospital, where she was greeted by sheer chaos, doctors yelling and blood and broken people everywhere. Gurneys with bodies—only a few hastily covered with a sheet—were stacked up on both sides of the hallway. In a room off the main lobby lay more bodies on pallets with arms and legs twisted and askew. "I had never known that blood could be so bright red," Betty would later say.

Most of the doctors had headed for Pearl Harbor as soon as the first bombs hit, so it was all hands on deck and no time for questions. Betty helped out in the emergency room, where she bore witness to some of the first American victims of the war.

"Bodies were laid on slabs in the grotesque positions in which they had died," she wrote. "Fear contorted their faces. Their clothes were blue-black from incendiary bombs."

Over in the corner, she spotted the body of a little girl around the same age as the boy she had pinched. She was barefoot and wore a red sweater, and had been jumping rope on a quiet Sunday morning when the attack hit. The rope was mostly gone, but her hands still gripped the charred wooden handles.

It was a detail that Betty never forgot.

* * *

Two hours after the initial attack, almost 2,400 American civilians and military personnel were dead, 21 ships were destroyed, and 164 planes were obliterated.

In a matter of minutes, the island of Oahu—and the United States of America—had morphed into a different world.

By nightfall on December 7, martial law had been declared throughout Hawaii and residents were essentially thrust into life in a war zone: Windows were blacked out to prevent attracting enemy gunfire at night, food and gasoline were rationed, and curfews and other restrictions immediately took effect.

The island's men flocked to sign up for military service, including Alex, who had served as an officer in the Naval Reserve for several years. Indeed, his unit was called up, and he reported for duty by the end of the week.

After helping out at the hospital, Betty headed for the newsroom and started cranking out her story. She wrote what she had witnessed: the chaos, the blood, the death, and the lingering threat in the air. But two days passed without her story in the newspaper, so Betty knocked on her editor's door.

Riley Allen had been editor of the *Star-Bulletin* for almost thirty years and had been instrumental in pushing for statehood for Hawaii from his first day at the post. Though the *Star-Bulletin* didn't publish a Sunday edition, Allen, an inveterate workaholic, was at his desk as usual on that fateful Sunday morning. The city was without a newspaper that morning since the presses at the *Advertiser*—Alex's paper—had broken down over the weekend. Allen saw the biggest scoop of his life and called in his reporters on their day off to hit the ground running. As a result, the *Star-Bulletin* would publish three extra editions before nightfall, and its eyewitness accounts would be republished around the world.

While he championed the truth in his pages, he drew the line at Betty's story. "I decided not to print your story," he told her. "I think it would be too frightening for the women to read this."

She argued that it wasn't any more graphic than what thousands of women on the island had already witnessed firsthand, but Allen held firm.

He wasn't entirely to blame. Though the US government would set up the Office of Censorship twelve days after Pearl Harbor, newspaper editors were already reviewing reporters' copy with an eye toward not revealing anything that could be used by the enemy. Plus, the military had already instituted a strict censorship program hours after the attack, which covered radio broadcasts and newspapers and magazines, as well as letters and other correspondence sent through the postal service. First-person accounts in any form were particularly scrutinized.

Indeed, in the frenzied days that followed, editors operated on sheer adrenaline, still in shock, printing wire stories about the attack as well as news briefs by local reporters, though few carried bylines.

So Betty traveled the island, talking with residents and sniffing out stories that she thought would pass the acid test. When she wasn't working eighteen-hour days for the newspaper, she helped set barbed wire along Waikiki Beach to supposedly keep the Japanese from invading.

She had wanted change and excitement . . . but perhaps not this much this soon. She did know one thing: She wanted to serve her country and help win the war. She especially wanted to go overseas, to see the war unfold up close.

But first she had to write a column telling housewives that using cheap cuts of meat like liver and lamb neck was a matter of national security.

* * *

Betty's choice of profession, though unusual for the time, hadn't surprised anyone. After all, when Elizabeth Sebree Peet was born in Washington, DC, on March 1, 1915, she joined a family with deep literary roots.

Frederick Tomlinson Peet, her paternal grandfather, was a renowned chronicler of the Civil War, with several published books of correspondence and memories. Her father, William Peet, was a longtime newspaperman, and her mother, Jessie Lydia Sebree, had worked as a reporter at the *Washington Herald* in addition to teaching high school English. In those days, newspapermen—and they were mostly men—frequently moved in order to move up even just one rung of the ladder. Betty's brother, Frederick, was born in Ohio two years after Betty, and two years after that, her sister, Marjorie, was born in Pittsburgh.

When her brother came down with tuberculosis, her father looked for a job in a more temperate climate, so when the sports editor slot at the *Honolulu Advertiser* opened up in 1925, the Peets headed to Hawaii.

Young Betty took after her parents and loved to write from a very early age. "I'd sit up in a big banyan tree and write all kinds of stories in my little notebook," she remembered years later. "And then I'd hide them."

She also loved history. "I was always fascinated with what had gone on before and what might be coming up," she said.

And she was fascinated with *who* was making history as well. After interviewing sports figures who were in town, her father often invited them to stop by their house at 903 11th Avenue, not far from Diamond Head. Betty already considered herself to be a reporter of sorts, so she'd practice her interviewing techniques on them in her living room. Walter Johnson, a pitching legend who played for the Washington Senators between 1907 and 1927, often dropped by. "He'd put me on his knee and we'd sit there and talk baseball," she said.

In fact, she was well on her way to becoming a published writer: Her first byline appeared in the *Star-Bulletin* in 1927, a poem titled "Hibiscus Blossoms."

She attended the Punahou School, an elite private high school where she was a star student, and her favorite subjects were English literature and history. She played on the girls' basketball team and covered girls' athletics for the *Oahuan*, the school yearbook.

The 1931 *Oahuan* described her "as the originator of nine-tenths of the deviltry perpetuated in study hall and classroom . . . she confronts irate teachers with an abashed grin, stoutly maintaining her innocence."

She couldn't wait to get out into the world: She skipped ahead a couple of years and graduated from high school in 1931, when she was only sixteen. But first came college. The country was deep into the Great Depression, but Betty and her family were somewhat insulated by it; her father had a good, steady job—when times are tough, interest in sports tends to increase.

Plus, Oahu and the other Hawaiian islands were less affected by the severe economic downturn than the mainland. The temperate climate allowed residents to grow their own food year-round, and the sugar and pineapple industries flourished in the 1930s due to booming exports, providing the island with low unemployment and a thriving economy.

Betty enrolled at the University of Hawaii in the fall of 1931, and threw herself into her studies and extracurricular activities. She joined the university theater guild and had a role in *Uncle Vanya*, and played Miss Whippet in Christopher Morley's drama *Where the Blue Begins*. She was also active on the women's tennis team, and in 1932 started writing sports stories for her father at the *Honolulu Advertiser*.

After her sophomore year, she traveled to Hong Kong before transferring to the University of Washington, where she majored in journalism and worked at the *Washington Daily*, the university newspaper. Growing up in Honolulu, Betty had been exposed to several Asian cultures and she wanted to learn more about them, so she signed up for Japanese language classes at UW. She graduated in 1935 with a BA in literature.

After graduation, she moved back to Hawaii to work for her father at the *Advertiser*, but she wasn't crazy about being a sports reporter; she wanted to write about people from all walks of life. She transferred to the features department, where her beat was to cover the waterfront. She loved it.

"It was great fun because all kinds of people were coming [to Honolulu] on boats in those days," she said. She frequently interviewed celebrities who were performing in Honolulu, including Groucho Marx, Mickey Rooney, and Jack Benny. And just like her father, she liked to invite her interview subjects home to continue the conversation.

Occasionally, a subject would hint that there was more to the comings and goings of the hulking naval ships docking at Pearl Harbor than met the eye, before letting it drop. Indeed, Betty had noticed more troops heading to the Philippines, and even the Red Cross was ramping up staff. Given the increased activity at the waterfront and in the city, most residents sensed that something was brewing. But she was supposed to focus on the lighter side of the news and save the hard stuff for the male reporters.

One day, not long after she had switched to features, she struck up a conversation with the reporter at the next desk over. Alexander MacDonald was on the police beat, and soon Betty looked forward to hearing his stories about crime and corruption in the city. He also shared her interest in Asian culture, and had traveled around the Pacific Rim before settling in Honolulu.

They soon became an item, and they were married on July 3, 1937. Marriage was good for them, both socially and career-wise. Not long after their wedding, Alex was promoted to Sunday editor of the *Advertiser*, and Betty moved over to the *Honolulu Star-Bulletin* to take a job as society editor.

Her salary was fifteen dollars a week—less than half of what many men doing the same job were paid. Betty had grudgingly accepted this, but she hated that female reporters rarely got raises. "It annoyed me because I had worked there for quite a while, and I felt like we weren't getting anywhere," she said.

She and Alex started building a life together and thinking about the future. They both dreamed of becoming foreign correspondents in the Far East, preferably Japan, and set about becoming proficient in the language. They knew total immersion was the key, so they moved in with a local Japanese family. Professor Saburo Watanabe and his wife, Keiko, owned a small language school on Oahu, and Betty and Alex dove right in, speaking nothing but Japanese once they walked through the door.

While they were living with the Watanabes, they hired an up-and-coming architect named Philip Johnson to build their dream house on a beautiful knoll nearby on a two-acre lot at 5960 Kalanianaole Highway, between Koko Head and Diamond Head.

Betty also started freelancing for the *San Francisco Chronicle*, filing a regular column, A Letter From Honolulu, to report on upper-class society life on Oahu, everything from weddings to who was entertaining house guests from New York for the weekend, along with gala events and celebrity fundraisers. She always signed off with "Aloha, Betty MacDonald."

Betty and Alex spent several happy years working hard, socializing with friends, and practicing their Japanese. The only thing missing, in Betty's mind, was a dog, but they had a cat named Skeets who acted like a dog, so she couldn't complain. Life was pretty perfect.

And then, on December 7, 1941, everything got blown to bits, including, eventually, her marriage.

*   *   *

A few weeks after the attack on Pearl Harbor, Alex reported for duty with the Navy and shipped out for points unknown. He never had another byline at the *Advertiser*.

Betty was sick with worry about her husband, but she buried herself in her work; after all, what else could she do?

She continued to report on the waterfront, but her focus had shifted: Instead of interviewing celebrities, she spoke with people who were arriving in Oahu by boat either to work or enlist. One day she interviewed Lieutenant Howell M. Forgy, a Catholic priest who told her of one time when he was traveling with a group of soldiers and their boat came under attack. He mentioned that the men ferried ammunition from one end of the boat toward the other side where the guns were stored. When the priest jumped into the line to help, one of the men shouted at him to stop. "He yelled back, 'Praise the Lord and pass the ammunition!' and I wrote that up," said Betty. In 1942, songwriter Frank Loesser would use her story with that quote to write "Praise the Lord and Pass the Ammunition," which bandleader Kay Kyser recorded and which hit number two on the music charts in late 1942.

Of course she knew her editor at the *Star-Bulletin* might well decide that the story she was working on would be too distressing to the women readers she was supposed to be writing for. But she believed her words were important, even if the powers that be didn't agree. So she approached her editor at the *San Francisco Chronicle*, which had published her lighthearted columns on social events in Oahu, and pitched a series of firsthand reports on how life had changed on the island since December 7, 1941.

He agreed, and she began to write the hard news stories that she couldn't publish on her home turf. The story "She Watched the Bombing of Honolulu" ran, with her byline, on December 13, six days after the attack.

Her words were finally getting out there, not watered-down reports about cheap cuts of meat to serve when food was in short supply. Plus, the *Chronicle* stories were being picked up by papers all over the country.

Her first bylined story in her home paper since the attack— exploring how local art establishments were storing their art in case of another attack—didn't appear until a full month after the attack. It wasn't hard news, but it was an improvement. She wrote one story about a local doctor who invented a machine to detect shrapnel in patients, and another on the "souvenirs" that locals were collecting on local beaches in the aftermath of the attack. But soon Betty was back to writing the same fluff pieces as before. In one article about spring fashion, published just two months after the bombing, she grudgingly wrote, "The newest spring suits will be collarless with cardigan fronts which will show off to advantage the print blouses with big bows tied under the chin."

Even her reports for the *Chronicle* regressed into old, familiar territory, covering weddings, births, and parties.

She felt frustrated. Her skills were being wasted. She still wanted to head overseas to become a foreign correspondent, just as she and Alex had planned, but she was completely stuck. And to make matters worse, she was essentially living in lockdown.

When Hawaii was placed under martial law just hours after the attacks, the military assumed total control, dictating daily life for residents. They closed bars and taverns as well as schools.

It was an everyday occurrence to check for your gas mask before leaving the house. Fingerprinting of all residents was mandatory, ostensibly for identification in case of death but also for registration purposes. Everyone was required to be vaccinated against typhoid and smallpox. Gasoline was scarce, so people couldn't drive anywhere.

Entire neighborhoods took on the look of shantytowns as families moved all of their household possessions and furniture onto lawns and sidewalks for fear that stray bombs or shrapnel would set their houses on fire. Other families headed for the mountains, believing it was better to hide out in the dense forests.

There were shortages of everything, and store shelves were bare, except for sugar and pineapple from the island's sprawling plantations. Shipping routes between islands and from the mainland had been shut down, so sugar and crates of fruit accumulated.

Everyone was jumpy, nerves were raw, and no one knew what would happen next.

Sometimes, in the frenzy of those days, Betty would think back to that little boy in the shop whose arm she'd pinched just hours after Pearl Harbor was attacked. Where was he now? And what had happened to his parents?

In those first fragile days and weeks after the attack, she could never guess that the way that she tweaked the truth of the boy in the rubble would turn out to be her ticket overseas and the path to independence.

Chapter 2

Zuzka

As a native of Czechoslovakia, Božena Lauwers, née Hauserová, was not a citizen of the United States on December 7, 1941, but when the Japanese bombed Pearl Harbor, her life would be altered just as much as Betty's.

After all, she'd had a bit of a head start when it came to hating the Nazis. Božena was born on April 22, 1914, in Brno, a small city in the southeastern part of the country, about 120 miles from Prague, the capital of what is now the Czech Republic. Brno was a mill town, and Božena's father, Karel, ran a factory that turned wood into furniture and flooring, which generated enough income to provide young Božena and her older brother, also named Karel, with a nanny, a cook, and a gardener. Despite the family's prosperity, their lives were not without tragedy. She was given the name of a sister who had died while her mother, Olga, was pregnant with her.

Her mother didn't have much time or energy for Božena; it was clear that she was still mourning the loss of her firstborn daughter (the fact that the two girls shared a name likely did not help). To mitigate her grief, Olga turned away from Božena and toward her son.

"I was closer to the nanny than my mother because my mother was very strict," Božena recalled years later. "She would always point out the negative stuff [we did]. I can't say that I feared her, but she used to dispense physical punishment. My father never did and neither did the nanny."

Božena was a sensitive child, attuned to the moods of the adults around her. She may have unconsciously reasoned that if her brother earned her mother's attention because he was a boy—and her mother didn't like girls because they might die—then maybe she should act like a boy, too.

She and Karel played with the other kids who lived in company housing at the mill, and Božena always led the way when it came to exploring places where they weren't supposed to go. She liked to jump on the carts that ferried wood between the buildings and sometimes had to cajole the other kids to come with her.

Božena often got into fights with her older brother, and she was the instigator more often than not. Their mother would break up the fight and then beat them with a wooden spoon. While Karel screamed and cried, Božena was stoic, showing no emotion or tears, grimly pressing her lips together until it was over.

When Karel went to school and talked about the things he was learning there, Božena couldn't figure out why she couldn't go yet, too. Once she was old enough to start school, she loved to learn and was a quick study, but she often got into fights—with the other students as well as with her teachers—and frequently questioned why things had to be a certain way, especially when girls weren't allowed to do the same thing as the boys.

Her parents led an active social life, and they loved to entertain. By this time, a sister named Olena had joined the family, and the nanny largely raised all three kids. When summer arrived, Božena was sent away; one year, she went to camp in Switzerland, and the following summer—despite the fact that Božena's father was Jewish—she lived at a convent with a group of German nuns.

She was fine with being away from her family. Božena was always up for an adventure, and she was always curious to learn something new. It was almost as though she went out of her way to do the things that scared others.

Before she was out of her teens, she had become fluent in German and French, and took eight years of Latin and four of Classical Greek at the city's elite high school, where she was one of only a few girls to attend. She graduated from high school in 1933.

Though many of her female classmates were engaged to be married by the time they graduated high school, Božena had no desire to settle down. The last thing she wanted to do was live the unhappy life of her mother; she had a brain and she was determined to use it.

She plunged wholeheartedly into life. She moved to Paris and spent a year studying at the University of Paris. She also splurged on a motorcycle and roamed the cobblestone streets of the city at all hours. A few men pursued her, but many more shied away at the prospect of being involved with such a forthright woman.

After a year in Paris, she wanted to pursue a profession. She considered going to medical school, but quickly ruled that out. "I was too squeamish at the sight of blood," she said. She returned to Brno and enrolled in law school at Masaryk University, where her brother had studied, and where she was one of only a handful of women enrolled in the program. On November 11, 1937, she graduated with a doctor of law degree and took a job at a law firm in her hometown.

She handled a variety of cases in civil and criminal court, but the work bored her and she left after just six months. A friend told her about a job in the advertising department at Bata Enterprises, a shoe factory in Zlín, which wasn't far from Brno. Despite the fact that she'd never worked in advertising, Božena figured that it had to be more exciting than working in a law firm. She applied, the company hired her, and she started her new job in the spring of 1938.

Though Zlín was somewhat looked down upon by Brno residents as being a bit of a backwater town, Božena found her circle of colleagues at the shoe company to be quite cosmopolitan: They hailed from different parts of Europe, and even the United States, and she loved the diversity because she was able to learn something new from every one of them.

She'd been working for Bata for about nine months, and though she liked her job and her coworkers, she was ready for a change, which arrived as a result of a bottle of apricot brandy that her teetotaler father had given her as a Christmas present. "You can add it to your tea," he told her.

While Božena didn't much care about what people thought of her and her unconventional ways, she also didn't want the staff at the hotel where she was living to think she was a drunk. So one night she invited her friends to her room to help her drink it. One of them begged off, that he couldn't make it, but maybe a friend who was visiting could go in his place?

"Sure," she told him. "He'll be able to taste an honest-to-god Czechoslovakian juice."

Like Božena, that visiting friend—Charles Lauwers, a Belgian-American who worked for Bata in their Czech and Senegal branches—loved languages; he was fluent in English, French, German, and Czech. They started talking in Czech and didn't stop for five days, when he and Božena announced that they were engaged to be married.

They set a wedding date for March 21, 1939, but her parents strongly objected, suggesting that perhaps a summer wedding would be more appropriate, the subtext being that one or both of them would change their minds by that time. Then, on March 15, 1939, Germany invaded Czechoslovakia, with Hitler riding into Prague in a red Mercedes to take a victory lap. Tens of thousands of citizens headed for the border to leave for other European countries or the United States, Charles and Božena among them. However, there was a problem: With his American citizenship, Charles was allowed to leave, but as a Czech citizen, his fiancée couldn't . . . unless they were married.

On March 16, they walked into the nearest church, said their vows, and then went straight to the American embassy in Prague. The city was a mob scene, with German soldiers already posted on every corner. The embassy issued Božena and Charles papers that would allow them to leave for the Belgian Congo—now known as the Democratic Republic of the Congo—where he would head up the Bata office.

Years later, she would admit that she barely knew him.

* * *

The trip—a quasi-honeymoon of sorts—took almost two months as they traveled across Europe with stops in Brussels and Paris before embarking on the ship that would carry them to their new lives.

At first, Božena viewed living in the small town of Léopoldville in the Congo as yet another adventure, but the thrill quickly wore off after they arrived. For one, Charles had to work much longer hours than he had been initially promised; the supply chains had been increasingly cut off by the encroaching war, which meant that he had to spend hours each day fixing broken machines and teaching employees how to make shoes by hand in addition to his regular responsibilities.

Božena's only responsibility was to care for the household, but since a cook and other domestic workers came with the house, she had little to do. Worst of all, she wasn't being intellectually challenged. So after spending yet another afternoon doing little more than smoothing the blankets on the bed, she decided to create her own opportunities. She contacted a few newspapers back home in Brno and offered to become a correspondent, filing travelogues and other articles for their pages. They agreed, and soon she had an excuse to travel around the region and talk to people for her stories. She also volunteered at a local hospital as well as the British consulate. But it still wasn't enough.

When Nazi Germany invaded Poland on September 1, 1939, the Axis blockade along the African coast became totally impenetrable: Nothing could get in or out. Charles thought the best solution was to buy new and refurbished machines from the United States and personally escort them back via a cargo ship disguised as a United Nations vessel, a strategy the Germans were already using to lay mines along the coast.

By this time, Božena was getting tired of following her husband's lead. She didn't want to be stuck in Léopoldville any longer and decided to accompany Charles to Cape Town, South Africa, from which he left for New York in December 1940. He said he'd be back in three months, and told her to wait for him. But as before, with a full household staff and the country at war, she had little to do. She continued to file a few articles for the Brno newspapers, and she at one point was so bored that she even tried to enlist with the South African army, which flatly rejected her.

Shortly after he touched down in New York, Charles discovered that his plan to buy machinery and ship it back to the Congo wasn't viable since American factories had already, long before Pearl Harbor, turned their focus to producing machinery for the war effort; a shoe factory in Africa was low priority. So he dropped the plan after three months and told Božena to head to the US instead. She landed in Hoboken, New Jersey, on April Fools' Day in 1941.

They found a small house to rent on Long Island and settled in. Compared to the small cities she'd lived in, Božena found New York overwhelming with its bustle, noise, and crowds. And though she knew enough English to get by, she was far from fluent. So while Charles worked at the New York branch of Bata, she freelanced at a local Czech paper along with a few small typing projects at the consulate. When they weren't working, she and Charles hung out with a large community of Czech expats who had also escaped the Nazi invasion, attending soccer games and doing a fair bit of socializing.

Though she was happy to be out of harm's way, her thoughts were never far from her Czech countrymen back home and how they were valiantly fighting the Nazis. She wanted to do something to help support them, but she didn't know what she could do when she was living thousands of miles away.

Then, just as a bottle of apricot brandy had set her on her current trajectory, a soccer game in New York set her on a totally different path. In November 1941, she and Charles were sitting in the bleachers with some Czech friends when she ran into Jan Masaryk, an old acquaintance from Prague who was then serving as the minister of foreign affairs in the Czech government-in-exile in London. After a quick catch-up, he got straight to the point:

"Why are you wasting your time bumming around in New York?" he asked her. "Off with you to the embassy in Washington, we need people, and *now*."

The consulate in Washington needed staff to help Czechs who had left as well as those who had stayed behind to resist and fight, he explained, and they particularly needed writers who knew their way around the law. Božena was thrilled: She was a perfect fit. She told Masaryk that she'd leave the next day, but Charles put his foot down. She was his wife, which meant that her main job was to support him and stay by his side, even if she was bored to tears.

Reluctantly, she told Masaryk that she couldn't go to Washington. But two days before Christmas—two weeks after Pearl Harbor—Charles enlisted in the Army Air Corps. With her husband gone, Božena could do what she wanted to do for a change. She headed to DC, where she took a job as ghostwriter for the press attaché at the Czech embassy.

Finally she was doing something to help her fellow Czechs. More importantly, she was out from under her husband's thumb and able to call her own shots once again.

Masaryk was right: There was a *lot* of work at the embassy. As ghostwriter, she wrote speeches, papers, and reports, and with every word she knew she was helping.

Since Czech was primarily spoken around the office, her English remained pretty rudimentary. Her coworkers—mostly male except for one harried secretary—were focused on their work, of course, and Božena liked the Czech camaraderie and culture that surrounded her every day.

This was also where she was first christened Zuzka, short for Zuzana, or Susan. It wasn't her name, but somehow it stuck.

* * *

At the embassy, in addition to serving as the primary ghostwriter, Zuzka also wrote the monthly reports for the military office, providing updates for the 310th Czechoslovak Fighter Squadron, which was part of Britain's Royal Air Force. Colonel Alexander Hess, a Czech fighter pilot, headed up the office, and he regularly invited her to the officers' club to play tennis or go for a swim, which was a welcome respite from the restrictions and rationing of wartime Washington.

One day in the winter of 1943, when Zuzka had been in Washington for about a year, Colonel Hess started to reminisce about the Battle of Britain, which had been a pivotal victory for the UK in 1940. In addition, it was the first battle ever to be fought primarily in the air, not on land. The battle, which staved off a German invasion of Great Britain, lasted three and a half months from summer into fall, and eighty-eight Czech pilots participated in the battle. Colonel Hess suddenly announced that he wanted to write a book about the battle. He turned to Zuzka: "And you will write it for me!"

She already had more than enough work on her plate, but she was flattered that Hess thought enough of her writing that he believed she could write an entire book. So she said yes to a project that morphed into an incredible challenge.

"I started writing something I had absolutely no knowledge of," she admitted. "And Hess was a man of few words. Every one of his sentences had to be stretched into a paragraph, often into a whole page." He was also occasionally unsympathetic to those who had not experienced the atrocities of direct warfare. "Many times he put me down when my description of aerial combat deviated too far from reality," she added.

She had to squeeze in the project after she'd finished her work for the day, and occasionally a coworker at the embassy reprimanded her for using electricity after hours during a time when everything from food to energy was strictly rationed in the nation's capital.

But as she wrote, she found herself filled with pride for what Czech patriots accomplished, albeit mixed with grief over their loss.

"Many times as I wrote and rewrote, I broke down crying over my countrymen, lost or maimed," she said.

Three months later, *We Were in the Battle of Britain* was published to positive acclaim in book form after first being serialized in a Czech newspaper in New York. Colonel Hess had the byline—not Zuzka, nor did the book credit her—but she didn't mind in the least. She believed she had accomplished something important and helped attract attention to the plight of her countrymen, even in a small way.

Not long after the publication, a new employee started working at the embassy. He was of Czech descent but had been born in the United States, and since he was twenty-six years old, the letter to draft him into the US Army soon arrived. He told the head of the embassy that he would rather serve in the Czech army, and Zuzka typed up the letter to the US Department of War as part of her regular duties. About a week later, he received permission to serve in the Czech army, but then he said he changed his mind and declared he would be better able to serve while working at the embassy.

"There was a huge ado in the office," Zuzka later said, the various administrators and employees all yelling at the man who, when pressed, admitted that he didn't want to fight at all, in either army.

At the time, the branches of the US military had made up posters that said "Free a Man to Fight," encouraging women to sign up for the women's branches of the Marines, Army, Navy, or Coast Guard. Women weren't sent into direct combat, so if a woman enlisted in the military, she'd be able to take a job in a support role that a man had been handling. Zuzka had seen the posters, which were plastered all over the city. So when everyone in the embassy was yelling over the guy's refusal to enlist at all, Zuzka stood up and said, "If he won't join the army, I will."

The men scoffed at her announcement, but the more she thought about it, the more it made sense. She would indeed be freeing a man for combat, and she thought it would bode well for her marriage, thinking that if she was in the military just like Charles, "it would surely help to bring us together after the war," she said.

Plus, she hoped it would get her out from behind a desk. "I didn't want to spend years pushing papers in Washington," she said.

"I hoped the service would be a great adventure which I did not want to miss," she added.

She resigned from her job at the embassy, and the next day she headed for the district court to apply for American citizenship, which was required before she could enlist. The rule didn't apply to men, only women. Zuzka didn't think it was fair, but then again, this wasn't her country . . . until now.

When she went to the Army recruiting station, the officer scanned her application.

"What kind of name is Božena?"

"A common Czech name," Zuzka replied.

"Not anymore," the officer said as she crossed it out. "You'll have to sign your name many times in the Army and you'll hold up everybody by spelling it. Why don't you adopt an American name like mine? Barbara. It begins with a *B* and ends with an *A* just like yours, so in the Army, you'll be Barbara."

Zuzka bit her tongue, raised her hand to take the oath of enlistment, and signed on the dotted line, assuming another name for the second time in as many years. An hour later, she joined the Women's Army Corps, and later that afternoon, she was on a train to Daytona Beach, Florida, to attend basic training.

Chapter 3

Jane

Jane Smith-Hutton was never good at standing still.

As the wife of a naval attaché, Jane lived with her husband, Henri, and young daughter, Cynthia, at the American embassy in Tokyo in 1941, which satisfied her zest for adventure. Like Betty, Jane loved Asian culture, particularly anything Japanese, so she was thrilled at the opportunity to immerse herself in Japanese art and culture and achieve a near fluency in the language. She even won several awards for her skills in Japanese brush painting.

Life at the embassy was exciting and rich, with diplomats and guests dropping by, and the several dozen employees came from a variety of backgrounds. Jane also relished her family's vibrant social life, forged over two years with embassy parties as well as through eight-year-old Cynthia's friends and their parents. But by mid-1941, lavish embassy dinners had become increasingly difficult to pull off due to dwindling supplies and bare shelves at the market from Japan's ongoing war with China.

Essentials like rice and cooking oil were in limited supply, and many stores and food businesses were forced to shut down as the government started to commandeer everything from ovens to printing presses to convert into iron for the war effort.

Jane and the other embassy wives and employees coped as best they could, frequenting back alleys where black markets for food and household staples operated, as well as placing orders to be shipped from a San Francisco wholesaler. By late November 1941, however, as life in the capital became more difficult to navigate, with frequent blackouts and increased police surveillance—all squarely aimed at foreigners—the embassy population had decreased significantly as nonessential staff members and most wives and children returned to the United States. Even Jane's Japanese friends had stopped dropping by since the military police made a regular practice of interrogating any Japanese citizen seen leaving the embassy premises, sometimes for hours on end. Ultimately, only a skeleton crew of sixty-four remained, including Jane, Cynthia, and Alice Grew, the wife of Ambassador Joseph Grew, who had become one of Jane's closest friends. Alice felt obligated to stay in Tokyo with her husband; plus, she wanted at least one American woman around for company. Fortunately, Jane had no qualms about staying in Tokyo, and Cynthia liked her school and classmates at the School of the Sacred Heart.

On the morning of December 8—Tokyo is almost a full day behind the United States—a team of Japanese military police barged into the embassy compound, ordering all residents not to leave the premises for any reason. Staff radio operators turned to their shortwave radios for any scrap of news to explain the sudden crackdown. One station reported that Japan had bombed Shanghai, which was entirely plausible due to recent news stories boasting that the Japanese army had made great inroads into China over the last few weeks.

One of the radio operators burst into the ambassador's office, his face ashen. According to a broadcast from a San Francisco radio station, Japan had bombed Pearl Harbor; another station had confirmed the shocking news. After embassy staff took a moment to absorb this information, they stood up en masse and headed for their offices. There was no question about their next move.

In an all-hands-on-deck frenzy, the staff grabbed every vaguely sensitive file, folder, telegram, and scrap of paper they could stuff into briefcases, boxes, and pockets before running down several flights of stairs to the parking garage, where they crammed everything into trash cans, doused the papers with kerosene, and struck a match. Then they ran upstairs for more.

As years of secrets burned in seconds, the lights overhead flickered briefly before the embassy went completely dark. A few minutes later, a screaming knot of military police forced their way inside and pushed toward the communications room, grabbing radios and pieces of transmission equipment as they went. They even pulled the wires from the walls.

They fanned out into the individual offices and ransacked desks and shelves, snatching any stray papers left behind. Some of the embassy staff pressed themselves against the walls to witness the desecration, while others retreated to their quarters so they didn't have to watch. After what seemed like hours, the MPs finally left the premises, arms overflowing with equipment and paper.

The raid had taken less than an hour. The long-anticipated war had finally begun.

* * *

Jane Ming was born in Globe, Arizona, on October 19, 1912, and from the way she lived her life, it seemed like she was always trying to escape the memory of that small mining town about ninety miles east of Phoenix.

Her childhood was far from blissful. Her father, Marcus Aurelius Smith Ming—who was of Welsh descent, not Chinese—joined the Arizona National Guard in 1910. He married Jane Ellen Thompson—who went by Ellen—in April 1912, and Jane was born six months later, with her sister, Mary Louise, following the next year. In 1917, Marcus became an officer in the Army and was soon deployed to Germany. After the First World War ended in 1918, he spent time in France before serving with the US occupation army in Germany.

While Marcus was overseas, his wife and two young daughters lived with Ellen's family in Globe. It was not a peaceful existence:

Jane and Mary Louise constantly fought, while Ellen was an alcoholic, prone to dark periods of depression, who felt stuck in Globe while her husband was in Europe. Plus, young Jane was sickly, and Ellen's maternal tendencies were few and far between.

By 1919, Ellen had had enough. She applied for a passport for herself and Mary Louise—but not for Jane—and took off for Europe to visit her husband at a military base in Germany. Young Jane had mixed emotions. She was glad to be free of her sister and her mother, but she was jealous of the fact that the other members of her family were off on a grand adventure. Plus, she desperately missed her father. Fortunately, her grandparents turned out to be better caregivers than their daughter, and Jane thrived as a result. Her grandmother loved to read and encouraged Jane to explore art, drawing, and painting, which she took a clear interest in. But without much opportunity or encouragement for literature and the arts in the dusty mining town, Jane could only pursue those interests so far.

Jane's peaceful existence lasted until 1923, when her parents and sister returned to the States. The Ming family bounced around a bit, first living in Stockton, California, before moving to Tacoma, Washington, where they lived at Fort Lewis.

At Stadium High School in Tacoma, Jane joined the Beaux-Arts Club, whose objective was to "further the interest, appreciation, and education of its members in various phases of art," according to her high school yearbook. Home life was still chaotic and unpleasant, and while Jane missed her grandmother, she didn't miss small-town living. After she graduated in June of 1930, she headed for Eugene, Oregon, where she enrolled at the University of Oregon.

Jane Ming had never subscribed to the then pervasive belief that just because she was a woman she couldn't do anything a man could do . . . or more. But reality quickly set in; the hardships of the Great Depression were firmly entrenched by the time she began her freshman year, and she struggled with her studies. She was also intensely curious about the world, and despite her unhappy home life, she fully recognized the benefits and opportunities for travel that the military provided. So a few months after starting her freshman year, she married Milton Johnson, a naval officer she had met in Tacoma, at Fort Lewis, on January 1, 1931. Like many women of the era, Jane viewed the marriage as a means to an end: It would satisfy her desire to travel and live in an exotic place while allowing her to continue her college education.

After the wedding, they immediately left for the Philippines, where Johnson was scheduled to deploy. But Jane didn't mind being alone. In his absence, she rented a small apartment in Manila, enrolled in classes at the University of the Philippines, and even traveled to China by herself several times.

By all accounts, the marriage was a disaster even though Milton spent most of the time on a ship somewhere in the Pacific. After one of his leaves, Jane discovered she was pregnant, and while she didn't want to stay married, she also knew she couldn't support herself, let alone a child, during the depths of the Depression. In late 1933, she headed back to the United States, moved in with her parents—who had moved to Iowa City in the interim—and filed for divorce.

Cynthia was born on April 23, 1934. Though Jane and her mother still didn't get along, at least living at home provided her with built-in childcare, which was fortunate since motherhood wasn't Jane's primary interest. She enrolled at the University of Iowa, where she studied composition, history, art, and home economics. But soon Jane began to explore other possibilities and larger cities.

Southern California had several military bases, and with a population of 1.3 million, Los Angeles was a sizable city with a mix of cultures and a significant university. Jane also figured that people in LA would care less about the fact that she was a single mother than people in small towns, where tongues incessantly wagged. So she moved to Los Angeles in 1935—the same year her divorce was finalized—and enrolled at UCLA, where she took classes in journalism, psychology, art, and literature.

But life as a single mother in the depths of the Depression was tough. Despite the demise of her first marriage, Jane was smart enough to realize that the only way out of her situation was to marry the right man, preferably a military officer who could provide her with some status and degree of financial comfort so she could continue her studies, along with a way to travel the world.

In 1936, she moved to San Diego; some friends of the family lived in the city, and perhaps Jane thought they could provide some moral support and occasional babysitting. Plus, there was a sizable Navy base in the city, with many more suitable marriage prospects than in Los Angeles.

When she wasn't in class or studying or spending time with Cynthia, she gravitated toward the bars and clubs that naval officers liked to frequent. It didn't take much to take a shine to Jane, a statuesque blonde with a brain that she didn't hesitate to use. But Jane was clear-eyed about the fact that many eligible men would consider a small child to be a detriment.

When she met Henri Smith-Hutton in San Diego, she immediately set her sights on him. A career naval officer, he alternated serving on ships in the Pacific with working as an attaché at the US embassy in Tokyo, where he had become fluent in Japanese. When he and Jane met, he was about to return to an extended posting on the USS *Lawrence* in the Pacific.

His leave was scheduled a few months later, and when his ship came into port in Seattle from Tokyo, Jane strapped Cynthia into the front seat of her car, a bottle perched on a pillow beside the toddler, and drove straight through from San Diego to Seattle to see him.

After a whirlwind few days—with toddler Cynthia in tow—Henri headed to Washington, DC, and Jane returned to San Diego. He was obviously smitten, and two months later, on June 10, 1936, he arrived in Norfolk, Virginia, where he met Jane and Cynthia before they headed for Sioux City, Iowa, where they were married on June 26, 1936.

The wedding announcement in the June 28, 1936, issue of the *Sioux City Journal* was unusual because the bride was listed as Mrs. Jane Ming Johnson, rare for the time as it indicated that she was previously married.

The newspaper reported that Jane "cut her bridal cake with her husband's sword." After the wedding, Jane, Henri, and Cynthia left for San Francisco in order to board the SS *President Hoover*, which was leaving in July for Shanghai, where Henri was to serve as communications officer on the USS *Augusta*, the flagship of the US Asiatic fleet.

Three weeks later, they arrived in Tsingtao, China, an international resort at the time, a quiet place where people could forget their problems for a little while. After spending a few days getting his new family settled into a small rented house with a garden, Henri headed back out to sea. As before, Jane didn't mind; there was a whole new culture to learn about and explore. She also loved to garden and kept a couple of chickens in the yard.

But Henri didn't want to be away from his family. This was his first marriage, and he was determined to be a good husband and father. So in February 1937, he transferred to a new job on dry land as an intelligence officer and moved into the small house in Tsingtao. His presence had a calming effect on Jane, and despite the fact that they had spent a total of maybe three months together since they had met, their relationship appeared to be compatible.

In addition to speaking Japanese fluently, Henri also dabbled in Russian, German, and French. He also liked to read Mother Goose stories to Cynthia before bedtime. As before, Jane appeared to be fine with relinquishing most of the parenting duties to someone else, and at least in this case, Henri was more than happy to shoulder the responsibility.

Tsingtao largely escaped the tension that was building in much of China in the late 1930s as the Japanese army continued to build up troops throughout the country. By the end of 1937, the Japanese had fully occupied Beijing and Tientsin, and the US Navy implemented evacuation plans for Jane and approximately two hundred other family members living in Tsingtao at the time.

Despite the threat of imminent danger, Jane and the other wives of military officers and consulate staff carried on as usual. She frequently hosted luncheons, often followed by hours of bridge. The spouses of local Tsingtao officials also came to Jane's social events, and while they knew enough English to participate in the conversations, Jane viewed their visits as a way to help her learn to speak a bit of Chinese.

By the spring of 1939, Henri learned that he would be transferred to Washington, where he would serve in the Office of Naval Intelligence. He and Jane were preparing for the move when a last-minute opportunity came up for Henri to serve as naval attaché at the US embassy in Tokyo. While many military families would have been happy to head back to the US after three years away, both Jane and her husband preferred to stay overseas. He accepted the position, and they arrived in Tokyo a week later.

The Smith-Huttons moved into a four-bedroom Western-style house adjacent to the embassy. It was a neighborhood where French and Italian diplomats also lived, and Jane was happy to live within an enclave of foreigners. The house had to be suitable for entertaining, since attachés customarily entertained frequently. Jane was happy with the sizable garden, and she quickly made friends just as she had in Tsingtao. She appreciated Henri because he respected her intelligence, unlike her first husband, who had wanted her to be satisfied with living a more traditional woman's role of housewife. Henri also confided in her . . . up to a point. They had to watch what they said around the house and on the phone, though. "The house was probably bugged," said Henri, "so we were careful not to discuss confidential matters."

Jane immersed herself in the new culture, but she faced more challenges in Tokyo than in Tsingtao. For one, food and household items had been in short supply for years, due to Japan's encroaching war in China and the stockpiles the Japanese government were creating in case of war with the US and/or Russia.

By 1940, Jane was throwing fewer parties, and not only due to the food scarcity. The US government started to pressure embassy staff in Tokyo to send family members back to the States during this tense and turbulent time. And as the Chinese army began to encroach on other regions of China, the US Asiatic fleet had also departed from Tsingtao, their former home.

As the summer approached, the writing was on the wall in terms of future military engagement with Japan. In May 1941, President Franklin Delano Roosevelt declared an "unlimited national emergency" in the United States, designed to empower the government to do whatever it took to prepare and protect its citizens in wartime, both at home and overseas.

By summer, life in Japan was becoming increasingly arduous. An article published in the *Cedar Rapids Gazette* on July 31, 1941, underscored the difficulties that Jane and the others at the embassy were increasingly facing. "The life of foreigners in Japan lacks the ease once associated with residents in the Far East," wrote reporter H. O. Thompson. "The Japanese police are constantly checking on foreigners, providing annoyance, irritation, mental or physical discomfort." The supply chain became even more squeezed, as matches, rice, and water were rationed, and public transportation became overcrowded and more perilous because both the human and mechanical resources to fix overburdened trains and streetcars were in short supply. Perhaps, for most embassy staff, the most apparent sign of constriction was that "there is no more imported whiskey in Japan, and foreign cigarettes and tobacco have disappeared."

Information was also hard to come by since newspapers and magazines were heavily censored by the government. One weekend in the fall of 1941, Henri and Jane took a short train trip to Hiroshima, the site of a large army base, so he could pick up a few clues about Japan's military plans, but they were trailed by a policeman the entire time. When the train stopped, the attendant pulled the shade down in their berth and told them to keep it lowered.

Shortly after they returned to Tokyo, the US Army ordered all officers to leave the country.

* * *

In the aftermath of the bombing of Pearl Harbor, the initial chaos at the embassy soon devolved into an eerie calm.

While Henri and his colleagues were busy dousing papers with kerosene, Jane and Cynthia were at home, nervously sitting in the dark and cold, since power had also been cut off to their house. Jane wrapped her fur coat around her daughter to keep her warm.

At dusk, a Japanese policeman knocked on the door and told them they had to leave. The officer scooped up Cynthia and carried her to the embassy. Jane followed behind, trying not to let her panic show. Once she was inside, one of six guards stationed at the embassy on twenty-four-hour watch locked the embassy gates from the outside.

The Smith-Hutton family and more than sixty others were being held captive by the Japanese inside the US embassy.

When Henri and the others updated her on the raid, Jane was outraged. She immediately stormed outside and recognized one of the guards as someone she had previously chatted with about where to find the freshest back-alley fish. Using her perfect Japanese, she cajoled him, offered bribes, and otherwise tried to reason with him, but he remained stone-faced, gesturing with his rifle for her to go back inside.

Henri, Jane, and the others started to ponder various likely scenarios about the length of their captivity. The one they landed on was that they'd likely be held for just a few weeks; surely they'd be released in time for Christmas. Given the growing shortages of food and everything else over the previous year, the embassy had recently placed a large order for food from a San Francisco supplier, which had arrived in November, so they had at least enough coffee, canned ham, and vegetables to last that long.

As the only family in the embassy, the Smith-Huttons moved into Ambassador Grew's one-bedroom apartment. Cynthia was in third grade at the time, and Jane homeschooled her as best she could.

As Christmas approached with no release in sight—and no communication with the outside world since their radios had been confiscated—their supplies started to run low. Jane took it upon herself to keep everyone's spirits up, for the sake of the others as well as for Cynthia. But it was a constant struggle. After all the years Jane had spent learning about Japanese language and art and culture—and all the good friends she'd made—she couldn't help but view their internment and the Japanese attack on Pearl Harbor as a personal betrayal.

The embassy staff celebrated the holiday as best they could, with a spruce tree from the garden strung with popcorn and carols sung around the battered embassy piano. Santa Claus even showed up, played by an Army language officer named Gould, who everyone called Pop.

On New Year's Eve, with no release in sight, they grimly accepted that they had to settle in for the long haul. Since they had diplomatic immunity, the Japanese knew that they couldn't beat them or hurt them in any way. The only option was to starve them.

The winter of 1942 was particularly severe in Tokyo. Fuel oil was running low, so the staff voted to use the limited energy supply to heat water for baths and laundry instead of heating the building. Jane and the other women cut up the embassy's curtains to make enough jackets and scarves for everyone.

Jane couldn't stand being idle, so she took charge of the daily routine at the embassy and decided the perfect way to keep everyone's spirits up was a daily poker game in the dining room since it was the only room with a fireplace; they burned food cartons, papers, and even furniture to keep warm.

They played Bach and Chopin records on the phonograph, and on Sundays, they sang hymns together; the last song was always "America." The liquor ran out on February 1, 1942. The tobacco held out for a few more weeks, and after that, the smokers resorted to putting coffee grounds in their pipes instead.

Jane was an avid amateur photographer, and had frequently taken pictures on her previous travels to China and when she was living in the Philippines. She was determined to document their confinement, and she shot rolls of film capturing candid scenes of her colleagues and the conditions under which they all were living.

The only contact the Japanese allowed them to have with the

outside world was Mr. Hausherr, the Swiss minister to Tokyo at the time, who had first been allowed into the compound ten days after Pearl Harbor was bombed. Hausherr became their lifeline, filling the captives in on news of the war. First he delivered warm clothing and bedding to the embassy, and then he convinced the Japanese to return one of the radios taken during the raid. They were also allowed to receive newspapers again, though both Japanese- and English-language versions were heavily censored.

With these few concessions, Hausherr began to negotiate for their freedom, which would require a diplomatic exchange of Japanese civilians who had been held by Americans since the onset of the war.

On June 17, 1942, Jane, Henri, and the others finally walked through the embassy gates after being interned for six and a half months. They boarded the *Asama Maru*, a Japanese ship, and were joined on board by US, Canadian, and South American civilians, missionaries, teachers, businessmen, and diplomats who had shared the bad luck of being in the wrong place at the wrong time. After being moored in the harbor for a week, the ship finally set sail on June 25.

Despite their internment in the embassy, the Smith-Huttons and their colleagues had been treated relatively well—or at least left alone, for the most part—at the embassy. Once they boarded the *Asama Maru*, Jane saw just how much worse it could have been. Her concern over the few gray strands of hair that had sprouted during her captivity vanished when she saw proof of Japanese brutality in the other passengers, who had been held in Japanese prisons and detention camps: the journalists who had been starved and tortured, a group of nuns who had been beaten and raped, along with many others.

"It filled me with a very great hatred of the Japanese when I saw maimed, undernourished and mentally ill people who came aboard, many of them old friends," said Jane after she was back on American soil.

As soon as the ship started moving away from Japan in the middle of the night, Jane headed up onto the deck to watch the lights of Japan fade into darkness as they headed toward freedom. She couldn't help herself and jumped up and down in her excitement. "Let's wake everyone up!" she yelled.

But the others advised caution. After all, the Japanese were still watching; plus, the harbor was heavily mined, so there would be no cause for celebration until the *Asama Maru* was out in open water.

Some took the time on board to decompress, but as usual, Jane needed something to do. One day, as she was walking around on deck, she noticed a small Japanese boy who had an infectious skin disease. She knew from her years spent in tropical climates that it would spread quickly unless treated. She took him to the ship's doctor, who refused to treat him. But she stood her ground and informed him that she wasn't leaving until he took care of the boy.

On July 23, 1942, Jane and the other passengers were overjoyed when the *Asama Maru* arrived in Portuguese East Africa, today known as Mozambique, where the exchange would take place. They'd be out from under Japanese control for the first time in almost eight months. The *Gripsholm*, a Swedish ocean liner, had gathered up hundreds of Japanese diplomats and civilians from throughout South America and the United States for the exchange.

As the crew maneuvered the two ships to facilitate the transfer of the *Asama Maru* passengers to the *Gripsholm* and vice versa, Jane stood on deck keeping a wary watch. Rumor had spread that spies and anti-war missionaries wanted to board the ship, which would eventually land in the US, and some of the rescued embassy crew were on the lookout during the exchange. At one point, Jane spotted a well-known American anti-war missionary standing on the pier, near an access ladder to the *Gripsholm*. He was chatting with a Japanese man, and Jane yelled down to them to get away.

"We have every right to be here," they shouted back.

"I'll show you how much right you have!" she said, swinging her purse around as she ran toward them.

"Fortunately," Henri recalled years later, "she didn't catch them."

Jane also helped Henri perform a little undercover work aboard the *Gripsholm*. A Chilean reporter rumored to be partial to the Japanese military had boarded the ship during the exchange, so Henri and Jane had devised a plan. The day before the ship was scheduled to dock in Rio, Henri searched the reporter's stateroom while Jane stood watch at the door. It didn't take long before he found a roll of thirty-five-millimeter film tucked inside a small tube that shaving soap of the time came in. He tucked it into his pocket, dug through a few more toiletry items, and ducked out before the reporter returned to the room.

Henri's find was significant. The roll of film came from the Japanese military, and the photos showed Japanese troops partying after their victories in Vietnam, Singapore, and the Philippines. The reporter had obviously been bribed in exchange for the promise to publish them, and if the photos appeared in Chilean newspapers, they'd quickly spread, first throughout Latin America and then all over the world. "It would have made all of the Allies look weak and harm the Allied cause," Henri explained.

Despite burning most of the embassy's documents back on December 8, Henri and the other staff members had held on to a secret stash of files that were too important to destroy, and had hidden them in various parts of the embassy after their confinement began. Now he had to get them back to the United States without detection; Japanese law at the time prohibited any foreigner from bringing any papers, newspapers, or magazines out of the country, and he knew he was a prime target for a search . . . but not his wife.

Jane had always traveled with at least nine or ten suitcases, and the years spent traveling through Asia and her various posts were no exception. So the day before the prisoner exchange, they divvied up magazines and papers between her clothes, tucking some into the lining of her suitcases to avoid detection.

Jane was thrilled that she was able to help prevent a potential disaster, and she liked being in on secrets. It gave her a taste for more.

* * *

Now transporting the prisoners freed from Japan, the *Gripsholm* arrived in Rio on August 10, getting ever closer to the United States.

Newspaper and radio reporters from all over the world had traveled to Rio to interview the detainees about their internment, and Jane spoke with several of them, happy that the story of their ordeal would receive wide coverage. When she mentioned to a reporter from *Life* magazine that she had taken pictures at the embassy over the past six months, he perked up and asked to see them. He offered to publish them, and the resulting article, "Americans Return from Jap Prison Camps: American Diplomats Held in Tokyo Lived in a Virtual State of Siege," appeared in a two-page spread in the September 7, 1942, issue of *Life*, featuring ten of her photographs.

Jane couldn't wait to set foot on American soil, though her elation was tempered by the knowledge that her remaining days with Henri were limited. After all, a military officer with his combined skill set of diplomacy and Japanese fluency would certainly be dispatched to the front during wartime. Indeed, when the ship arrived in Rio, Henri received orders to fly immediately to Washington.

He debarked from the ship and stood on the pier as Jane and Cynthia waved to him while the *Gripsholm* pulled away. As the dock faded from sight, Jane didn't know when—or if—she'd ever see her husband again. She felt so betrayed by the people of a country she had loved.

Jane vowed to get even.

Chapter 4

Marlene

In the late 1930s, Marlene Dietrich's glamorous movie career had hit the skids, a stunning fall from grace since she had first found worldwide fame with *The Blue Angel*.

Less than a decade after that landmark film, not only had moviegoers' tastes changed, but American studios were churning out too many films with little attention paid to quality, resulting in dull story lines and uninspired acting. Theater owners across the country regarded Dietrich and other top names of the day—including Joan Crawford and Katharine Hepburn—as persona non grata in an effort to influence the studios to make more profitable films.

The feeling was mutual: Marlene had long felt unchallenged by unimaginative directors and dictatorial studios that just wanted her to rinse and repeat the sultry siren roles she had long ago mastered. These days, she was far more worried about the devastation that Hitler and the Nazis were inflicting upon her native Germany—especially her beloved Berlin, where she first became a star and where her mother and sister still lived. But the last time she had been to the city was in 1933—when Hitler came to power—and Marlene had vowed to not set foot in her homeland again until the Nazis were gone. "I shall probably never again make films in Germany," she said.

She even helped establish a relief fund to help Jews and other exiles escape from Germany with director Billy Wilder, who left Europe for Hollywood in 1933, by donating the $450,000 payment from her starring role in the 1937 film *Knight Without Armour*.

Despite this, the Nazi propaganda machine relentlessly pursued her, offering her millions of dollars to star in their films, where she'd work alongside the esteemed director—and Nazi darling—Leni Riefenstahl. Marlene wasn't the only target; as the Nazis took hold, they launched "Home to the Reich," a program to entice Aryan Germans who were living abroad to return home for the good of the Fatherland. Joseph Goebbels, the chief architect of the Nazi propaganda program, set his particular sights on those Germans working in the entertainment industry in the United States, and obviously the bigger the name, the better.

Goebbels adored Marlene, and her return to Germany would have confirmed his vision that Nazi Germany filmmakers— including Riefenstahl—were superior to those in Hollywood. He watched every one of her movies several times and did everything he could to entice her into moving back, including sending her a Christmas tree from the Führer himself.

To be sure, some Germans detested Marlene and had regularly picketed in front of theaters at her films throughout the 1930s, especially because many of the directors of her movies were Jewish. They believed that she'd been led astray, dazzled by the sparkling lights and money of Hollywood, and if only she returned to Berlin, she'd be able to acknowledge the error of her ways. Goebbels would have been happy if she agreed to act in just one of his movies.

But of course Marlene refused his offers. She was totally disgusted at the way the Nazis had taken over the country, and how her fellow countrymen and -women were kowtowing to Hitler and everything he and the Nazi Party represented.

"She loved the culture of Germany," said her daughter, Maria Riva. "When this country, with its culture and its beauty, was transformed into the personification of ugliness and cruelty, it was very difficult for her to accept it. She did not turn her back on her home-land, but rather on what it had become."

Just as Jane Smith-Hutton wanted to get revenge on the Japanese, Marlene wanted to hit back at the Nazis. "What people don't know is that I couldn't resist twisting the knife in the arrogant hearts of those gentlemen," she admitted. On June 6, 1939, Marlene declared the ultimate revenge when she renounced her German citizenship and officially became a US citizen—she had applied two years earlier—which created a huge ruckus in the media back home.

"The German film actress Marlene Dietrich spent so many years amongst Hollywood's film Jews that she has now become an American citizen," read the caption of a photo of her citizenship ceremony that was published in a Nazi newspaper. "Here we have a picture in which she is receiving her papers in Los Angeles. A Jewish judge . . . is taking from Dietrich the oath with which she betrays her Fatherland." And almost immediately after becoming a US citizen, Marlene didn't hesitate to publicly curse those Americans who wanted the United States to stay out of the war.

On December 8, 1941, the day after the Japanese attacked Pearl Harbor, when President Franklin Delano Roosevelt declared war on Japan, Marlene was a few weeks away from turning forty. Three days later, when the president announced that America would also be fighting the Germans, Marlene rejoiced. Finally, here in her adopted country, she'd no longer be going it alone against the Nazis. She couldn't wait to start helping in any way she could. But first, in the chaos of those first few days after infamy, she had a question for her fellow Americans:

What the hell took you so long?

*   *   *

Marie Magdalene Dietrich was born on December 27, 1901, in Schöneberg, Germany, the second of two daughters. Her family nicknamed her Lena. Her father, Louis Otto Dietrich, was a former military officer turned police lieutenant, and her mother, Josefine

Felsing, came from an upper-middle-class family of clockmakers. However, the marriage was not a happy one, and by the time Marlene was five years old, her parents had separated; her father still supported the family, however.

Tragedy would dog the family for Marlene's entire childhood. A year after Louis had moved out, he unexpectedly died, supposedly from syphilis. Josefine had two small children to support, so she hired herself out as a housekeeper to families in the same social circles that she had been born into. Josefine had learned the hard way that she actually had little purchase over her life, and as the daughter of a clockmaker, she saw the sense in using hours and minutes to bring at least a small amount of control into her girls' lives.

She instituted airtight schedules for Lena and Elisabeth, her older daughter, regulating everything from the precise amount of sleep to the time allotted to play outside. "My mother was like a kindly general," Marlene said years later. "She followed the rules she laid down and set a good example to prove that it was possible. No pride in success, no pats on the shoulder, the only goal was humble submission to duty."

* * *

Germany was a country that had long been in love with its military history. Many school holidays celebrated the anniversaries of war victories, and classrooms were often led by teachers who served in the army reserves, and who regarded their young charges as their own personal platoon, to be shaped into dutiful soldiers. With her mother's insistence on scheduling every minute of her day, Lena already had enough of this at home, but as a ten-year-old girl, her options for rebellion were obviously limited. So she decided to christen herself with a new name to separate herself from her family and her ultramilitaristic teachers.

"I wanted a name that was all mine, only mine," she said. She combined her names—Marie and Magdalene—into one, Marlene, and thereafter refused to answer to any other name.

"There was no one else named Marlene. I thought Marlene was a much more glamorous name."

It was her first official act of rebellion, with many more to follow.

∗   ∗   ∗

Marlene was an intensely curious student, and she threw herself into her schoolwork, French and English lessons with various tutors, and gymnastics. But her favorite activity was music, specifically the violin. She loved playing her instrument, and was soon playing virtuoso repertoire.

She was on the cusp of adolescence in 1914 when two separate events shook her world. First, her mother married Eduard von Losch, who had been Louis's best friend. Marlene's stepfather was an officer in the Prussian army and came from a family of aristocrats, which pleased the always status-conscious Josefine, not to mention the military discipline she had always been drawn to.

But perhaps even more life-changing for a young girl than a new father figure was when Kaiser Wilhelm II, the German emperor and king of Prussia, declared war against France, Britain, and Russia in August of 1914, assuring his citizenry that the war would be won in a matter of days, if not weeks.

German men trudged off to fight the enemy, including Marlene's stepfather and several of her uncles. But the Kaiser had grossly miscalculated the strength of the enemy, and German troops encountered strong resistance from their enemies almost from the beginning. Within a matter of months, towns and cities all across the country had been emptied of men, leaving women to do the bulk of the work.

Many of Marlene's male teachers and classmates had been among the first to leave for the front, which meant that instead of learning about math and history, Marlene and her female classmates spent their time knitting gloves and socks for the soldiers as the war dragged on. Food, fuel, and household goods were beginning to be in short supply. Many wives took over their husbands' jobs at the war's beginning, but as factories and businesses began to close, they started to stay home, albeit in unheated homes. Their daily diets consisted of turnips and potatoes and little else. School was canceled more often than not, due to the lack of heat, and the fact that the children were too weakened by malnutrition to be able to absorb their lessons.

Tragedy struck the family a few months after the start of the war when Marlene's beloved uncle Otto was shot and killed in December 1914. Eighteen months later, the family received word that Marlene's stepfather was killed on July 16, 1916, after suffering injuries on the battlefield.

Marlene had lost two fathers and a cherished uncle, all before she turned fifteen.

* * *

The war dragged on for over two more years.

Marlene spent her remaining teenage years with a black ribbon braided through her hair as a sign of mourning. Everywhere she went, she was surrounded by brokenhearted women, both at home and in the classroom on the rare occasions when school was in session.

Marlene escaped by going to the movies and writing in her diary. She felt like she had lost her teenage years and could never get them back.

"Why must I experience these terrible times?" she wrote in her diary. "I did so want a golden youth and now it turned out like this! If I were a little bit happy, things wouldn't be so difficult. Maybe soon a time will come when I will be able to tell about happiness again, only happiness."

She vowed that she would live the rest of her life in a way where she could make up for her lost childhood, to choose her own destiny and—most important—be happy.

* * *

In November 1918, when Germany capitulated and an armistice was signed, World War I was finally over.

But postwar life in Germany still looked a lot like wartime: There were shortages of everything from food to fuel, and citizens were still shivering and starving. To make matters worse, the Spanish flu had taken hold earlier in the year, and by 1919, an estimated one thousand people were dying each day in Berlin alone.

Germans, including Marlene's family, had long placed their trust in the government and the military, and after the war was over, it was clear that the country had failed them on every front. After more than four years of fighting an unwinnable war, Germans were disillusioned, and they were ready to try something different.

Marlene was ready to make up for the years she had lost, and against her mother's wishes, she decided not to go to college, or even finish high school.

She moved to Weimar in the fall of 1919 to pursue a career as a professional violinist. Weimar had a more active artistic and cultural world than Berlin, and she thought that a different city was the perfect place to start her new life. She diligently practiced for up to eight hours a day in order to qualify for a seat in one of the city's orchestras. But she developed a severe case of tendonitis, and was warned away from life as a professional musician in order to avoid any further damage. She moved back to Berlin to live with her mother while she figured out another way she could make her mark.

Marlene had always loved going to the movies, so she thought maybe she could become an actress. She took a few acting classes, and after talking with other women who acted with local theater companies and in silent movies, she began auditioning for parts, sometimes several times a day. She was quickly offered some small jobs, from dancing in a chorus line to singing in vaudeville routines and at smoky cabarets. She also did a bit of modeling on the side. A few small film roles soon followed where she played everything from a maid to a prostitute. A few reviewers had noted that she had the making of a great actress, and indeed, Marlene was perennially frustrated by the parade of minor roles that continued to come her way. She had always believed that she was destined for much greater things.

When she wasn't auditioning for stage work, Marlene was immersing herself in the risqué, anything-goes world that was the Berlin cabaret scene in the 1920s. "It was a splendid time," said Ernst Josef Aufricht, who would go on to produce Bertolt Brecht's musical play *The Threepenny Opera*. "The long, bloody war was over and had become a ghost."

Marlene—who had been attracted to both men and women since adolescence—happily flung herself into the city's nightlife, hanging out at both straight and gay bars and attending drag shows until dawn, often accompanied by her coworkers.

Then, in 1923, she did something that was totally out of character for her: Marlene got married.

Rudolf Sieber was an experienced assistant director who was frequently in charge of casting pictures for the renowned director Joe May. In late 1922, Sieber was auditioning Berlin-based actors for *Tragedy of Love*, a movie projected to be four hours long and co-starring Mia May, the director's wife. Due to the length of the film, financing was unusually substantial, and actors and actresses who were regulars on the Berlin theater circuit showed up in droves to try out for the movie, including Marlene. Though he initially cast her as an extra, Sieber saw something of the star in Marlene, and quickly upgraded her to a minor speaking role. Marlene was grateful for the part, but she surprised herself when she fell in love with Rudi; it didn't take long for him to follow. Barely six months after they met, on May 17, 1923, they got married. Marlene was twenty-one years old. Their daughter, Maria Elisabeth Sieber, was born on December 13, 1924.

After settling into family life for about a year, Marlene resumed her movie career, along with her previous freewheeling lifestyle. Both she and Rudi openly engaged in other romantic relationships— Marlene with men and women, and Rudi with women—and in fact his mistress became Maria's nanny, an arrangement that all were apparently comfortable with.

Marlene spent the second half of the 1920s much as she had the first half: pursuing acting gigs, some in films directed by her husband and others with rival directors. Most of the parts were small, but she never hesitated to jump on board as an extra, justifying it with the idea that she never knew who she'd meet and what they could do for her.

Everything changed in 1929 when she was cast as Lola Lola, a cabaret singer in a Weimar nightclub who has an affair with a local high school teacher, in the movie *The Blue Angel*. In the film, she sang the song "Falling in Love Again"—the song she would become most famous for—and her on-screen presence absolutely smoldered. Two versions of the movie were filmed, one in German and one in English; Marlene's language lessons had paid off. When the movie was released in 1930, it was an instant hit, first in Germany and then internationally, primarily due to her screen presence and a couple of things that were shocking for the time: First, in an era where most women never wore pants, on-screen or off, Marlene wore a tuxedo and a top hat.

But the more scandalous moment came when she actually kissed another woman on the mouth.

Word quickly spread and people flocked to the movie, and other countries negotiated for the rights. Paramount Pictures took notice and signed her to a contract for several Hollywood movies. *Morocco*, her first film at Paramount, actually came out a year before *The Blue Angel* was released in the United States. She again played a cabaret singer—this time opposite Gary Cooper—and was nominated for an Academy Award for Best Actress.

The next six years passed in a blur as she made ten more films, including *Shanghai Express* and *The Garden of Allah*, but Marlene had never been a big fan of the extracurricular activities actors were expected to do in order to remain at the top in Hollywood, from the press junkets to hobnobbing with other actors and actresses. "I've been invited to the house of Joan Crawford," she wrote to Rudi back in Germany. "*Unfortunately.* These parties are nauseatingly boring."

Acting was also starting to bore her. Marlene wanted to learn more about the technical aspects of moviemaking, so in the moments when she didn't have to be in front of the camera, she shadowed lighting directors and camera operators. She applied her new knowledge and began to take a more active role in shaping her film career in an effort to stave off the tedium that was never far away.

She was paid as much as $500,000 for each movie, an exorbitant sum at the time. But as the Depression dragged on, moviegoers wanted to forget their troubles and laugh at the movies, not necessarily be titillated by a sultry sex symbol. The box office take on her films started to plummet, and in early 1938, a group of independent cinema owners took out an ad in the *Hollywood Reporter* announcing a group of actors they thought were "box office poison."

Marlene was in good company; she made the list along with Joan Crawford, Fred Astaire, and Katharine Hepburn.

If Hollywood didn't want her, well then she didn't want Hollywood. Marlene was happy to return to Europe, flitting between London, Paris, and Austria. But she didn't stay away from the States long. As Germany began to forcibly expand its territory into Czechoslovakia, making another war more of a distinct possibility, staying in Europe wasn't safe. Despite her "poisoned" ranking, Hollywood studios and producers still wanted to make movies with her, and she moved back to California.

Just as quickly as her popularity had plummeted a couple of years earlier, it was resurrected in 1939, starting with the Western *Destry Rides Again* with James Stewart. Marlene played Frenchy, a singer in a down-and-dirty saloon, and was paid about half her previous fee. With no other prospects, she took the job, and the role jump-started her career.

And to be sure, becoming an American citizen didn't hurt.

But making movies was beginning to bore her; she wanted to do

something that made her feel fulfilled, like she was making a difference.

It took Pearl Harbor to find what she was looking for.

*   *   *

As an American citizen, on December 8, 1941, Marlene hit the
ground running.

In those first few precarious weeks after President Franklin Delano Roosevelt declared war on Germany, Marlene began plotting
how she could use her celebrity to help fight and defeat the Nazis she
despised for ruining her homeland. America had its own problems,
of course, but at least she was free.

Marlene continued to make movies—it paid the bills—but the
work became less and less fulfilling, especially when she saw what
other Americans were doing to support the war, including selling
war bonds so the US government could finance the war without raising taxes. Investors bought a bond at 75 percent of face value, which
could be cashed in at full value ten years in the future. Everyone
from children and housewives to celebrities got involved in encouraging others to buy bonds, and Marlene was the figurehead, touring
all over the United States for more than eighteen months, urging
her fellow citizens to buy war bonds. She appeared at department
stores, shipyards, and even movie premieres—not her own—to help
finance the war, and at each stop, she sang, kissed men and babies,
and signed countless autograph books.

Marlene also appeared at nightclubs, and she never passed up the
chance to sit on a few men's laps and get them drunk so she could
sell even more. When President Roosevelt got wind of it, he wasn't
happy and called her on the phone. "We're very grateful to you for
that," he told her, "but I forbid you to perform these salacious acro-
batics. From now on, you must not appear in any more nightclubs,
and that's an order."

She obeyed, and started to help in other ways, like appearing in
a national campaign to encourage women to donate their old silk

stockings, which would be used to manufacture gunpowder bags. She broke new ground in other ways, too. Ever since Marlene became famous for wearing pants, female employees at Hollywood movie studios had badgered their bosses for the chance to wear pants to work. RKO, Universal, and Paramount all initially rejected the idea, but the women continued their pressure campaign. Eventually the studios agreed, saving face by claiming cooperation with wartime restrictions dictated by the federal government. "Long skirts and unnecessary frills are out for the duration," stated an article in *Variety* in the spring of 1942. "The Office of Production Management in Washington warned producers to eliminate all wasteful use of dress material in feminine garments on the screen."

But like Betty, Zuzka, and Jane, Marlene never felt she was doing enough. "I'm not going to sit here, working away quietly, and let the war pass me by," she said. "I wanted to help in ending the war as soon as possible. That was my only desire.

"I have no illusions about the glories of war," she added. "I lived through one terrible war, and I knew that this one was far worse. [In America] I saw complacency. I couldn't do much, but I had to do *something*."

ACT TWO

GLORIOUS
AMATEURS

Chapter 5

Zuzka

If Zuzka thought that New York was a culture shock, basic training in Daytona Beach, Florida, was another type of whiplash altogether.

Her English was still shaky, and the other women in her unit teased her for it, not always kindly. "They called me DF, for Damn Foreigner," said Zuzka. "I ate like a European, knife in right hand and fork in left, and the other girls would just stare at me in the mess hall." One day a woman took personal offense.

"Hey you," she said, "grab the fork in your right paw and shove it in your face like we do."

Due to her limited English, Zuzka didn't grasp what she was saying. "I beg your pardon?" she asked.

"DF doesn't even know how to feed properly," the other woman muttered and returned to her meal.

There were other cultural differences, too. At basic training, all women received a maroon bathrobe made of corduroy. The other women complained among themselves at the quality of the clothing, but after growing up in a relatively impoverished country, Zuzka had a totally different take. "I thought it was sheer luxury," she said.

She wasn't embarrassed by her lack of proficiency in English; instead, the taunts from the other women motivated her to study the new language in earnest. Indeed, by the time basic training had ended, she had become so proficient that she was recommended for Officers Training School. She headed to Fort Oglethorpe in Georgia, but before the first day of class, she was sent back to Daytona Beach and ordered to receive more specialized training in advanced survival techniques, including marching for miles in the heat wearing full military gear and swimming through water where oil burned on the surface.

Zuzka figured that she was destined for some kind of secret mission but didn't know the extent. She and the other women training with her speculated about their fate, but when they realized that the one thing they all shared in common was that they were fluent in at least one other language besides English, they determined they would probably be stationed overseas.

When training was over, they were sent to Washington, where the secrecy continued. Zuzka and the other women were told to report to 2430 E Street, known as the Q Building, not far from the Lincoln Memorial and overlooking a brewery and a skating rink. Since she was in the Army, she was guaranteed a place to live, and moved into a rustic barracks with the other women.

On her first day in November 1943, she learned that she'd be working for the Office of Strategic Services, an organization she'd never heard of. "Nobody explained it to us, though we were told we were working for an elite group," she said. "We were told to mind our own business, don't ask any questions, and be available 24 hours a day, seven days a week. And if anybody asks us what we were doing, we were to say we were file clerks."

Immediately she was put to work in the OSS's Secret Intelligence (SI) branch as a translator. Her first assignment was to put documents into separate bins according to the language: "My job was to sort out reports in various languages," she said. "I'd identify the language—whether it was Slovene, Croatian, Serbian, or Bulgarian— and then file it."

Work began at eight A.M. and continued for twelve or thirteen hours, with a half-hour break for lunch. For this, she was paid the grand sum of twenty-five dollars a month, with room, board, and transportation included. She found the work boring and tedious, but figured that she had to prove herself.

Over the Christmas holiday in 1943, much of the city and military barracks emptied out. She spent a lonely holiday with a few other WACs who also had nowhere else to go. She thought of her husband, Charles, who corresponded only sporadically; it was hard to believe that they hadn't seen each other for two years. All she knew was that he was currently based in New Mexico waiting for his own travel orders.

She jumped at the chance to attend a New Year's Eve party at the Czech embassy in Washington, and when she showed up in her military uniform, the tongues started wagging.

"Some were malicious, others a bit envious," she recalled. She chatted with others—mostly in Czech—and speculated on the fate of their home country. But when anybody asked what she was doing in the Army, she smiled and replied with the standard line, "I'm a file clerk."

She wasn't lying—she *was* a file clerk—but Zuzka hoped that things would change before long.

The following month, she got her wish.

*   *   *

Zuzka's travel orders arrived in January 1944, and she transferred to Newport News, Virginia, to head overseas. She boarded a ship that was pointed east, so she figured she would be stationed in Europe, but she didn't know where.

The first stop was Oran in northwest Algeria, where Zuzka caught a train to Algiers, a French colony at the time, a customary first stop for OSS divisions before they went off to their assignments, mostly in southern Europe.

She was transferred to the Research & Analysis division as an analyst—no more endless filing—though her primary responsibility was to serve as French translator for her boss, H. Stuart Hughes, who headed up the R&A office. It was winter and bitterly cold.

Zuzka was long used to subpar accommodations, but the convent where she and the other OSS women stayed was far less than desirable: In the middle of an icy Algiers winter, there was no heat. "Never in my life was I as cold as I was in North Africa, but eventually spring came and my frozen ears thawed," she said.

"We stayed in the laundry room where the floor and walls were beautifully tiled, but icy cold," she said. "Each of us got two standard issue blankets that were heavy, hairy, and greenish brown, one to sleep on, the other to wrap in. We wrapped, but didn't get warm."

And they were fed, but again, the food was less than adequate, though Zuzka tended to view everything through an optimistic lens. "We were constantly learning something useful," she said. "I learned how to fry an egg on a small electric iron turned flat side up and flanked by three faces blowing on the egg to keep it from slipping off."

On the job, Zuzka juggled numerous tasks in addition to translating for her boss. OSS agents who were stationed behind enemy lines, as well as double agents, would radio in reports in a variety of languages: French, Italian, German. The radio operator would write it down as best they could and hand it to Zuzka, who would translate the garbled transcription and edit it into some kind of report for higher-ups.

She also learned how to decipher aerial photographs, writing up brief reports based on her analysis:

What do you see? A road.

What is on it? Traffic.

What kind? Tanks.

At what intervals? Four in a minute.

What direction? South.

Give a report in ten words or less.

The fact that she was a private—the lowest rank in the Army—never came into play. If they needed her skills, she jumped right in with a high degree of competence, and no one complained about her rank. "I was able to do what they asked me to do, thanks to the languages," she said.

But she couldn't help but look at the men in her unit with a little bit of envy: They were training to go where the real action was. She was attached to the 2677th Regiment, where most of the soldiers were paratroopers training with the 1st French Paratrooper Regiment as they prepared to go behind enemy lines.

It looked like fun, but more importantly, they were destined for something bigger. She convinced a few soldiers to show her how to jump out of a plane after hours at the training center. It turned out to be a disaster.

"I broke my collarbone and knocked out several teeth," she said. She couldn't tell the doctors how she had really got injured, so when they assumed she had gotten drunk and fell down, she didn't correct them.

* * *

Due to the extremely lopsided male-female ratio, the few women in the unit were expected to attend parties, dinners, and other social events. "We were supposed to, let us say, be of assistance to the officers," she said. "Whenever the paratroopers were to be dropped, there was a farewell party for them. We were supposed to supply the female element."

Which often meant sex. She shrugged it off more often than not, figuring that it was part of the job.

Since Algiers was a stopping-off point, lots of higher-ups passed through, and one day in the spring of 1944, General Bill Donovan, the head of the OSS, showed up. A party was arranged for that night, and every woman in the unit was informed that their attendance was required. At one point, Donovan pulled out his .45 and took aim at a piece of metal on the other side of a ravine. He took a few shots but didn't hit the target. Zuzka was standing nearby, so after he was finished, he handed the pistol to her and said, "Your turn, soldier."

The junior officers who were toadying around the general made a few wisecracks about girls who couldn't shoot as Zuzka took aim and pulled the trigger. When a sharp ping of pierced metal sounded out, they all turned to her.

"Donovan had a very benign smile," Zuzka said. "I opened the pistol, threw out the casing, handed it back to him, and made a quick exit. After that, everyone called me Sharpshooter."

It cemented her belief that she could be doing more than translating garbled radio transmissions and providing the female touch at parties. In May 1944, Zuzka was transferred from the Research & Analysis division to Morale Operations, which was a big step up since it meant that she'd be creating information instead of processing and deciphering documents prepared by others. Her facility with languages definitely helped, along with her background writing newspaper articles and books for the Czech embassy. It was around this time that she discovered that the OSS higher-ups had actually recommended that Zuzka transfer to MO back in September of 1943, commending her for her loyalty, ability, and personal character. But whether they wanted to make her prove herself first or decided to wait until the need for MO grew more acute is unclear. In any case, Zuzka considered the transfer a promotion, though she still retained the lowly rank of private.

The spring of 1944 was indeed the ideal time for MO to ramp up; after all, black propaganda worked best when civilians and soldiers were starting to doubt what their leaders were saying about the progress of the war. And the tide had recently begun to turn against the Axis powers.

When the Allies took Rome on June 4, 1944, followed two days later by D-Day, Morale Operations kicked into high gear. The entire OSS Algiers office moved to Rome, and Zuzka would finally get her chance to prove what she could do.

* * *

Zuzka and her twenty-two male coworkers were housed in a mansion that Mussolini had built for his mistress, and Zuzka immediately got to work. Her colleagues included Norman Newhouse of the Newhouse newspaper empire; William Dewart Jr., who published the *New York Sun*; and Saul Steinberg, an up-and-coming cartoonist who would later become famous for his work in *The New Yorker*.

While MO had previously been aiming propaganda at the German troops who had occupied northern Italy, their attention now expanded to include the civilian population. The team hit the ground running.

Zuzka and Steinberg became fast friends. Together they came up with an idea to make toilet paper featuring Adolf Hitler's face. The Rome MO office had access to a neighborhood print shop, but this project had to look crude and amateurish, like a civilian could have created it or a disgruntled soldier who had secretly turned against the Nazis. Steinberg carved out a picture of Hitler on a piece of linoleum with the words "*Diese Seite Benützen*," German for "Use This Side." They hand-printed a number of rolls and gave them to OSS agents to distribute in German jeeps and latrines.

One of their next projects was a fake newspaper called *Das Neue Deutschland*, or *The New Germany*, which German soldiers were led to believe was published by a peace and resistance movement inside the country. The front page of the June 15 issue juxtaposed recent Allied victories alongside failed German battles; as always, both stories were slightly exaggerated—victories were much larger and losses more overwhelming in the articles—but always crafted around one strong kernel of truth.

The newspaper was typically distributed by airplane drops, but delays were common and logistics nightmarish. Plus, newspapers were unwieldy, so *Das Neue Deutschland* was printed both in full size and as a miniature version that was more like a leaflet.

Postcards were also a popular device at MO Rome because the time frame for delivery was less urgent. Germans knew it could take weeks or months for a postcard or letter to show up in the mail since the transportation sector in the country was in shambles, from blown-up rail lines to roads pockmarked by shells. Zuzka and her colleagues wrote and hand-addressed postcards telling recipients that the war was futile. The cards were then stuffed into mailbags that OSS agents had stolen and smuggled back from Germany, and subsequently dropped by Allied aircraft onto bombed trains that carried the bulk of mail around the country. Unwitting rail workers then transferred the mail to the nearest post office. The problem was that with Allied aircraft ramping up their own sorties, it could take weeks—and numerous bribes—to secure a craft willing to go where you wanted it to go.

Two weeks after she landed in Rome, Zuzka was just settling into a routine when a golden opportunity fell into MO's lap. On July 20, 1944, there was a failed assassination attempt on Hitler's life. Despite the Nazis' fevered efforts to squelch the news, both German soldiers and civilians quickly learned about the botched attack. The time was ripe for MO to create the most devastating forms of propaganda possible.

The team quickly started batting around ideas to capitalize on the news, drafting a new issue of *Das Neue Deutschland* and writing and laying out several leaflets, including a proclamation from a top German field marshal who announced that he had overthrown the Reich and was now in charge, and asked both the military and civilian population to help him. This was printed on authentic German military letterhead that had been previously stolen by OSS agents. MO agents also printed and circulated a proclamation announcing that the high-ranking general Albert Kesselring had been instrumental in the attempt on Hitler's life.

Distribution had to be fast, as arranging for an aerial combat unit to drop the leaflets in enemy territory would take too long. Zuzka and the others decided that the quickest way to distribute the propaganda was to have German POWs cross into their native country, make the drops, and then return to Italy. It was a high-risk operation, and illegal as hell given the constraints of the Geneva

Convention, which prohibited POWs from being used for military purposes or "placed in positions of mortal danger." Not to mention whether a POW could be trusted to (a) return to Italy and (b) not divulge the details to the Nazis.

There were thousands of German POWs being held in Allied camps across Italy, and finding the best men for the job would be like looking for a needle in a haystack. They had to be native German speakers who could travel in the country without raising suspicions since they would be disguised as German soldiers. Since Zuzka was the only MO member who was fluent in German, the other team members decided that she would interview and select the POWs at an Allied camp in Caserta, 130 miles south of Rome.

"It was a farfetched idea from the very start," Zuzka admitted years later. "To send a female into a camp which housed thousands of prisoners was risky because I could have been done in right then and there, and nobody could have saved me because of the mere number of POWs against one woman.

"But in OSS we were fortunate enough that no matter what kind of an idea we had, we were told, 'If you think it will work, go ahead.'"

And since few outside of the OSS were aware of MO's existence, Zuzka and the others were confident about the chances of getting away with skirting certain aspects of international law.

They dubbed the program Operation Sauerkraut, and got to work. Guards and overseers at the camp initially screened the POWs, specifically selecting those who were against the war: They either had been involved in anti-Nazi action or sabotage of some sort, had been unwillingly drafted, or had family who had been imprisoned or killed by the Nazis. One week after the botched assassination, Zuzka and Captain William Dewart took an Army jeep and drove all night over rutted roads to Caserta to find their POWs.

* * *

To get around the ban on recruiting POWs to participate in war-related operations, MO had to turn it into a strictly voluntary action;

after all, there was no regulation that prevented POWs from *volunteering* to help their captors win the war. So before she began her interrogations, Zuzka's first question had to be "Do you want to volunteer to fight against the Nazis?" If the prisoner responded in the affirmative, and the prisoner acknowledged the danger they were entering into, the interview could proceed.

In each interview, Zuzka tried to inject a sense of ease into the process, making the prisoner feel that he could trust her. If he let down his guard, she could get a better feel for whether he really wanted to stick it to the Germans—and then return to the relatively comfortable POW camp, with three meals a day—or whether freedom was more important, and he'd be tempted to run once he was beyond the barbed wire and back on his own home soil.

After driving all night, she headed into the interrogation tent the British guards protecting the camp had set up and waited for the POWs to show up, one after another, almost like an assembly line. Most were initially hesitant, but the cigarettes she offered served to loosen them up. She had twelve hours to choose sixteen men before loading them up on an Army transport and heading back to Rome. The operation would begin the next day.

It was a delicate balancing act. Just like the POWs, she began each interview tense and coiled to strike. As the interview progressed, she relaxed a bit, but not too much. She followed a simple process of elimination based on her gut.

Then the guard brought in a man who appeared to be the Platonic ideal of a German soldier. "He was an absolutely beautiful specimen, tall, blonde, blue-eyed, and elegant," she said later. "But he was highly offended that a woman was sent to talk to him, and the first thing he said to me was 'We will show you what we can do, the Jew in the White House will be finished pretty soon, we are bombing New York.'"

With a few of the POWs, Zuzka liked to puff herself up to appear bigger than her full five feet two inches. But she didn't with this Nazi. "He was absolutely obnoxious and I just listened and let him go on for a while," she said. "I'm half-Czech and half-Slovak, and where I come from one Slovak equals five Irishmen when it comes to temper," she added to explain what happened next.

"Say that again, about Roosevelt." She brushed an imaginary piece of lint off her lapel.

He repeated his sentence word for word, never breaking eye contact.

She punched him in the jaw and heard something crack. "I gave him a knuckle sandwich," she said. "He was so stunned that he didn't do anything, just stood there wide-eyed, completely frozen."

The British guard poked his head into the tent. "Is anything wrong?"

"I'm through with that bloke," she told him as she tried to catch her breath.

As she waited for the next prisoner, she started to shake. The POW had not been handcuffed or restricted in any way. He could have rushed forward, jabbed a hard thumb into her throat, and it would have all been over in a few seconds.

"He could have done harm to me, but he didn't," she marveled years later. "He was just too stunned by my audacity."

* * *

While Zuzka was interviewing the POWs in Caserta, members of the Research & Analysis and MO teams back in Rome were busy rounding up enough uniforms and equipment for the POWs to wear for their foray into Germany. After all, the POWs had to be able to pass as real German soldiers, with uniforms, papers, and tools that could withstand close scrutiny. Everything from the helmets to buttons to boots had to be up-to-date, which was a real problem since the Nazis frequently changed the look of insignia and papers as the war dragged on and quality supplies became more difficult to source. Some of the POWs selected for the mission helped pitch in by making their own helmets and forging dog tag IDs with an anvil and hammer while rehearsing cover stories for their fake identities.

Just ten days after the assassination attempt, the POWs were driven into enemy territory, just to the north of the Arno River. Since the Allies had pushed the German army out of Rome, the Nazis had retreated to Florence, 170 miles to the north. The POWs not only had to keep an eye out for German soldiers patrolling the area but also had to watch every step since the region was peppered with landmines, booby traps, and barbed wire.

In addition to carrying adequate ammo and weapons, maps and compasses, and other necessary equipment, each POW also carried a gas mask and spare canisters, into which were stuffed three thousand leaflets or notices to be distributed in areas where German soldiers congregated.

The POWs fanned out in three separate teams in different directions. In addition to dropping the leaflets, they were also instructed to hide undercover after making the drop so they could witness soldiers' reaction to the propaganda along with noting their overall appearance and health.

They posted orders on trees, threw leaflets into German tanks and latrines, and even gingerly placed some beside sleeping soldiers. Then they retreated into the woods or inside abandoned buildings to wait.

They didn't have to wait long. As soon as a soldier read the leaflet or posted proclamation, he immediately showed it to another, which set off an animated discussion. In one instance, an entire platoon scanned the leaflets and yelled "The war is over!" before tossing their guns on the ground and running away from their station and toward the Allied-held line to surrender.

Whenever a German soldier gave himself up, Zuzka learned, the Allied soldier who greeted him unfastened his belt or suspenders before removing them. "He would then have to hold his pants with one hand, and that reduced his potential by half," Zuzka later noted.

Two days later, all the POWs returned unharmed, and as they were debriefed by the OSS, it was clear that the operation was an unmitigated success. The POWs needn't have worried about not being able to pass; in one instance, they were so convincing as German soldiers that they came under fire by a group of Italians.

Subsequent interrogations with German soldiers who surrendered to the Allies specifically pointed to the propaganda as their motivation for deserting. The conditions that the POWs witnessed also provided valuable intelligence that the OSS could pass along to its own agents in the field as well as use to map out future military strategy.

For instance, upon their return, a few of the POWs reported that the soldiers in the 4th Parachute Division were in low spirits due to lack of food, threadbare clothing, and rationed equipment. In fact, ammunition was in such short supply that commanders had instructed soldiers to hold their fire unless officers gave specific orders. With this information, Zuzka and the others had proof that German troops were in rough shape and would be more inclined to believe MO's propaganda.

While MO and OSS teams sifted through the information the POWs brought back, it was clear that Operation Sauerkraut would be repeated. But the POWs had to be rewarded for their efforts in some way, and Zuzka had come up with a novel, if not exactly legal, way to increase the odds that they would return.

In addition to their main office space, the MO team kept a safe house in Rome to use for clandestine meetings and other nefarious purposes. After the POWs returned from their mission, it was time to pay them as agreed. Zuzka drove the men to the safe house, where an MO colleague had made previous arrangements with some local "working girls." The POWs headed upstairs while Zuzka sat outside in a jeep doing crossword puzzles. After a few hours, the girls came downstairs and Zuzka paid them in Italian lire. "It was my chore to pay for the POWs' well-deserved pleasures after a successful mission across the lines, but I was wondering how this expenditure will be explained to the US taxpayer by the disbursing OSS officer," she admitted.

The line item for "Miscellaneous" was larger than many other categories in the MO budget.

"We were plain lucky," she said years later. "Not a single one of those fellows tried to escape and vanish into the Italian countryside. They could have spilled the beans to the other side, but they never did."

Operation Sauerkraut was an absolute triumph, with plans for repeat performances within weeks.

Zuzka was just getting started.

Chapter 6

Betty

Six months after the Pearl Harbor attack, Betty got her wish to get out of Hawaii. She moved to Washington, DC, to take a job with the Scripps-Howard News Service. Her beat: covering First Lady Eleanor Roosevelt during wartime.

Washington was a boomtown in mid-1942; a war economy meant the rapid expansion of government offices and that jobs were there for the taking. The country had barely emerged from the economic and social ravages of the Great Depression, so the sheer availability of jobs was especially important for marginalized populations, including women and racial minorities.

Between newcomers flocking to the city and military and support staff traveling to bases for training before heading overseas, it's estimated that two hundred thousand people a day were coming through Union Station during 1942.

As a result, the housing situation in the city was dire. Fortunately, Betty had an aunt living in the Georgetown neighborhood who rented out rooms, so she moved into a small room on the top floor of her house. It wasn't far from the newspaper headquarters, so she was able to walk to work, which was lucky since gasoline was in short supply due to rationing.

Betty settled into her job. In addition to articles on the First Lady,

Betty wrote a weekly column called Home Front Forecast that was syndicated to Scripps-Howard newspapers all over the country. In the majority of her work, her subject matter was once again along the lines of the best ways to use cheap cuts of meat in the wake of nationwide rationing and coupon books.

She recognized that she was providing a valuable service, but she was bored by the women's beat. Betty made up for the lack of challenge by roaming the streets of the capital in search of a good story beyond her beat. And she still dreamed of heading overseas to be closer to the action.

Once, she met Ernie Pyle in the Scripps-Howard newsroom. Pyle was a celebrated correspondent for the wire service who had spent several years traveling around the United States reporting about the everyday men and women who he met in the course of his travels. After covering the Battle of Britain in 1940, he was promoted to war correspondent at the wire service, and on his visits to the home office, he kept Betty and other reporters spellbound with tales of Europe and North Africa.

By 1943, Betty was growing restless. She still wanted to go overseas, but now she wanted to leave Washington as well. The city had started to feel stifling, and the heat and humidity of summer was overwhelming. In an attempt to soothe her itchy feet, she occasionally traveled back to Honolulu to file updated stories on how island residents were coping during wartime. In February 1943, she took a new job as feature writer for the Newspaper Enterprise Association, which broadened her horizons a bit. She hoped the job would lead to something more.

* * *

One day Betty got a tip about a man living in DC who had invented a machine to cut sugarcane. She was still writing occasional stories for newspapers back in Hawaii and thought it was a timely story, since most of the residents who worked in the sugar fields on Oahu had joined the military and labor was tight. She scheduled an interview with Atherton Richards, the inventor, and when she showed up, she discovered that he knew her father from back in Hawaii. She wrapped up her questions for the story, and they started talking about people back home they knew in common. She told him she and her husband had lived with a Japanese family in order to become fluent in the language.

He perked up and asked if she ever thought of working for the federal government.

"Only if they promise to send me overseas," she replied.

"I think we can do that," he said, and handed her an application.

Betty's natural tendency to ask too many questions vanished into thin air. There was no mention of what she'd be doing or which part of the government she'd be working for, but she didn't care. She had heard the magic word: "overseas."

Atherton Richards had recently become the executive assistant to General Donovan. The bureau was ramping up to hire thousands of people who were fluent in at least one foreign language, and Japanese was obviously in demand.

Betty was called for an interview a week later and offered the job. She gave her notice to her editor at the wire service, and on August 6, 1943, she officially became an employee of the OSS.

* * *

On her first day on the job, Betty reported for duty. She filled out some paperwork and was fingerprinted, and then settled in for orientation with her new coworkers, a much more eclectic bunch than her newspaper colleagues. They included a dog breeder, a radio show producer, a former Olympic champion, and a couple of Thai missionaries.

Detractors often joked that OSS really stood for "Oh So Social" or "Oh So Snobbish" due to the fact the majority of staff were recruited from the upper classes and members of the *Social Register*. But Donovan, for his part, specifically pursued this population because he thought they were less likely to succumb to bribery in exchange for state secrets. And of all the government agencies and branches of the military, the OSS had the distinction of hiring the highest proportion of women who had graduated from college.

Donovan wanted the most experienced people he could find, regardless of gender.

Betty was assigned to the Japan desk as a reporter, though with an important twist. She was used to thinking up and writing stories based on facts; in her new job, she had to create stories that *sounded* true but that contained small untruths. "We were taught how to get rumors started and to disseminate material, a mix of truth and fantasy," she said years later.

"As a newspaper writer I had been taught that everything had to be right and correct, and we were changing everything to make people think differently," she said.

She thought back to that little boy whose arm she'd pinched on December 7 back in Honolulu. It felt like a lifetime ago.

Here, in her new life, she'd essentially be doing the same thing, tweaking the news to get a reaction out of the reader.

The office resembled the newsrooms she was used to: one large—and loud—room with desks pushed together at awkward angles, providing plenty of space for tossing ideas back and forth. Typewriters clacked away, and piles of files and newspapers were stacked haphazardly on desks. Betty sifted through a mountain of top secret intelligence reports and cables from spies in the field alongside analyses about the status of the war in Japan and the countries and regions it occupied. She also studied black propaganda that was created by the British as well as the Germans and Japanese. Out of this massive influx of information, some ideas would float up, and soon she was reading correspondence and updates with an eye toward how the data and facts could be angled toward the Japanese.

Even better than the dry reports sent by diplomatic pouch from the field were actual documents and keepsakes, most often taken from the bodies of dead Japanese soldiers. Mail sent home was heavily censored on both the Allied and Axis sides, and so soldiers' true confessions in the forms of diaries, notebooks, and unsent letters offered up a goldmine of unfiltered thoughts. If they confessed on paper that they felt they were fighting an unwinnable war, Betty and the other propagandists could take that information and create a pamphlet or newspaper that appeared to come from pacifist organizations or resistance movements within Japan. She also sifted through dozens of new reports and communiqués that came in overnight.

Japanese newspapers and magazines were also particularly valuable since the MO writers and graphic artists could mimic the tone and appearance of stories. Another target audience of MO consisted of people who lived in countries occupied by the enemy, like wide swaths of China, Burma, and India at the time.

The propaganda that Betty and her cohorts produced often incorporated artwork, so she had to find cartoonists within the ranks of OSS staffers. She detailed the caption and any specifics she wanted to see in the cartoon to be reproduced.

"I am enclosing some pictures of cartoons of sumo wrestlers from Japanese magazines," she wrote in one order. "We will reproduce the cartoons as if the page had been torn from this magazine."

Every day she had various plates spinning: reading new intelligence reports, leafing through the pages of a waterlogged diary taken from the body of a Japanese soldier, and coming up with lightly twisted ideas for stories and pamphlets.

Though she loved the work and the frequently whacked-out ideas of her colleagues, Betty was becoming impatient with the slow pace of production at the MO office. After all, back at the *Star-Bulletin*, she was used to coming up with an idea for a story, interviewing sources, and writing it all in one day, to be printed the next day after a quick scan by her editor.

Plus, at the paper, she'd had a lot of autonomy. Of course she'd realized that any government office had many more layers of bureaucracy, but given it was wartime, she expected a bit more expeditiousness and speed.

In one missive, she wrote, "This is a rush job, which must get out to the field immediately, and I would appreciate if you would hurry it up."

But the gears of government bureaucracy have always turned at a glacial pace, even during wartime, and her work and that of her colleagues needed to pass through many pairs of eyes before it was sent to the field. Many more documents and print-ready files ended up in filing cabinets in DC than distributed in the field. In fact, the secretary in charge of filing all of the examples told them to slow down at one point because she was running out of space to put new filing cabinets.

To add to Betty's frustration, a year after joining the OSS based on the promise that she would be sent overseas, she was still stuck in Washington and facing the prospect of spending another swampy summer in the nation's capital.

She was beginning to despair of ever leaving American soil.

But June 6, 1944, changed everything.

* * *

On D-Day, the Allies launched the Normandy invasion to drive the Germans out of Western Europe, and two weeks later, the Allies crushed the Japanese in the Battle of the Philippine Sea, which destroyed 90 percent of the Japanese air fleet and led to the Allies recapturing Guam over the summer.

It was time to move MO operations closer to the action to make it easier and faster to distribute propaganda into the field.

On July 12, 1944, Betty received orders to transfer to the MO outpost in Kunming, China. Before she left, she spent several weeks in a mandatory training program, where she and other students would learn the skills they might need overseas, everything from handling firearms to learning the best methods to eavesdrop, tail people, and break into houses and factories.

In one exercise, an instructor led students into a room and told them to provide a profile of the person who lived there, including their job as well as a physical description, based on the objects found there. Betty thought it was fun, though she had a hard time trying to figure it out since her newspaper career had taught her never to make assumptions about anyone based on outward appearances.

In the next test, Betty helped a couple of men training with her to use long poles and wood blocks to assemble a building the size of a small shed. Her assignment was to convince them to put it together in a different way. But her powers of persuasion were lacking since in her previous occupation, she typically took a more passive role, listening to what other people had to say instead of telling them what to do. "I failed that completely," she admitted years later. "Afterwards, I was told that I should've picked up the pistol lying in the room and used it to make the men do what I wanted."

The instructors assigned each student a false identity and name in a test to see how well they could stick to their stories under pressure, as if they had been captured by the enemy. Betty's alter ego was a stenographer named Myrtle, an intriguing choice since she had no idea how to take dictation and wasn't a particularly strong typist. Again, her results were less than stellar: Another student assumed the name of Betty, and "Myrtle" reflexively turned her head whenever she heard the name.

In another exercise, students were instructed to use their fake identities to talk their way into local factories that were only open to employees, common at the time in wartime Washington. Betty headed to the Boeing Airplane Company near Baltimore, but instead of using Myrtle to gain access, she flashed her White House press pass at the door, telling them she was there to interview the head of the company. They waved her in and she wandered around a bit. "I didn't know what I was looking at, but at least I was in there," she said.

Next came training in firearms and explosives. Betty and her cohorts headed to the Congressional Country Club in Bethesda to learn how to throw grenades, fire machine guns, and drive a jeep. "The first time I fired a Thompson submachine gun it almost turned me around in a circle—the kick was so powerful!" she said. "But I got the hang of it."

After classes, the alcohol flowed freely in the evenings, but again it served as a kind of test. "There were a lot of drinking parties to see how we acted in social situations and how we behaved after drinking alcohol," she said.

Betty was a light drinker, so alcohol wasn't a problem. In fact, she liked to joke that she could get high from sniffing the olive from a martini. But then came the last night of school, when instructors encouraged their students to drink up with very liberal pours to see if their students were cut out for the pressures of an overseas assignment.

Many of them—including Betty—failed spectacularly as cover stories floated away and state secrets fell from their lips in proportion to the amount of liquor consumed. The next morning, Betty woke up with a pounding hangover. "I felt like a full-blown moron," she said, and thought she was at risk of being kicked out of the OSS, or at least permanently mired at her sweaty desk in DC for the duration of the war.

She returned to Washington fully prepared to clear out her desk and call her old editor and ask for her previous job back covering the First Lady, though she dreaded it. "I knew I'd have to write a straight news story again and be a civilized human being, and how dull that would be," she said.

She was amazed to learn that she passed all of her classes with flying colors.

* * *

On July 12, 1944, she flew from Washington to Miami to hole up at the Floridian Hotel for a few days before catching the first of several military flights to New Delhi.

She looked forward to having a few weeks to acclimatize herself in New Delhi before proceeding on to the post in Kunming, where

MO operations continued the specialty she'd honed back in DC: developing propaganda to demoralize Japanese troops.

But when she arrived, she was told that she'd be staying in New Delhi because the Kunming office was already fully staffed, which she knew was a lie. Betty called upon her ferreting skills from her newspaper days and quickly learned the real truth: The new American ambassador to China didn't want his wife to tag along with him, so to keep her in the States, he had issued a military-wide declaration that China was too dangerous for American women.

Though she was a bit disheartened, Betty could live with the situation: At least she was out of Washington. Her move overseas resulted in a raise in pay and classification from analyst/writer at $2600 a year to MO representative/operations level CAF-9 at $3200 a year. And she soon discovered that her job in the field would require much more than just writing articles and leaflets. She also had to think about the best way to get their "product" into the hands of their target audience.

Wartime rationing at OSS headquarters had been an issue that Betty and her coworkers accepted without question; after all, they all had learned to adjust to limited everything during the Great Depression. Once she arrived overseas, however, supplies were a different issue since it could take weeks or months for new stock from the States to arrive. "Every paperclip was saved and used again, and every pencil was counted before offices closed at night," she said.

While Betty and the other women appreciated that Donovan gave them free rein back in DC, it was a far different story in the field, where she was one of only two women at MO headquarters in Delhi. When she approached Colonel Harry L. Berno, the head of supplies at her new station, about the prospect of replenishing supplies, he wasted no time telling her that he thought women's wartime talents were better used back home wrapping bandages for the Red Cross.

After that, Betty approached him only when absolutely necessary, but a limited supply chain created huge challenges, since tiny nuances in the finished product could affect the authenticity of a printed piece of propaganda and whether recipients took it seriously.

For instance, Betty and her colleagues had to weigh when to use an offset printing press and when a letterpress would be better. "We couldn't use an offset press to produce newspapers or clippings," she said. "Even the most casual newspaper reader would sense something was amiss since letterpress type leaves a definite dent on newsprint, where offset makes no physical impression on paper."

The paper they used also had to be authentic. "Japanese newsprint was made from a coarser, cheaper grade than Americans used," she said.

In Delhi, in addition to creating propaganda aimed at the Japanese military, Betty and her colleagues also had to craft propaganda aimed at civilians who lived in regions that were occupied by the Japanese military, including China, Burma, and Indonesia.

Just as Zuzka had to get creative with a linoleum shard to create toilet paper with Hitler's face on it, Betty had to improvise out in the field. One of her projects was a leaflet directed at Indonesians, urging them to resist their Japanese occupiers and to perform acts of sabotage against them. Previous operations had distributed pamphlets from airdrops, but Betty didn't want to go this route because it would be clear the leaflets came from an Allied plane. The British equivalent of MO was also stationed in Delhi and occasionally cooperated with the Americans on operations and supplies. Betty had recently become friendly with a man in the British navy, and she asked him to help her by taking the leaflets with him by submarine and distributing them by essentially floating them into the country.

He agreed to the operation, but how to waterproof the leaflets? Balloons? No good, they were obviously in short supply. But condoms weren't. Betty asked the infirmary for five hundred condoms, and after a lot of questions and some raised eyebrows, they handed them over.

It was all hands on deck to inflate the condoms and slip in the propaganda—along with a much-prized antimalarial pill as an added inducement—before the British sailor took off in the submarine. Betty and a couple of colleagues were about halfway through the project when *"A-ten-shun!"* suddenly bounced off the cinderblock walls, and in walked General Donovan. He'd long made a habit of visiting far-flung OSS outposts to show his support, and liked to make surprise visits.

He walked into the room just as Betty had her mouth around the open end of a condom. "He took one look at us and what we were doing, smiled very faintly, then turned and left," said Betty.

Donovan took it in stride; after all, he had created his own monster by hiring people for MO who were kind of a ragtag bunch, and not commonly known for saluting when a higher-up walked into the room. Since Betty didn't enlist in the military when she joined the OSS, she was technically a civilian. However, she did have an Army uniform—sans insignia—to wear in case she was captured. "Then, they'd have to treat me as a prisoner of war," she explained.

In fact, Betty's lackadaisical attitude toward anything military got a colleague in trouble when he was promoted to sergeant and he asked her to sew on his insignia. "I sewed them on upside down because I thought they'd look better that way, and besides, that's the way the British did it," she said. "He got demoted for it."

*   *   *

There was another obstacle Betty faced when trying to persuade Japanese soldiers to give up. The Japanese had been indoctrinated from birth to never surrender, but instead fight to the death. If they gave up to the enemy, they'd lose their birthright and would be forever banned from their homeland. "We had to crack through the fanatical indoctrination he had received since childhood," she said.

One morning, at one of their daily planning sessions, staffers discussed news of a recent shake-up in the upper echelons of Japanese government, which gave Betty an idea: What if they were told that they *didn't* have to fight to the death? The timing was perfect to create a forged order—supposedly from the emperor himself—to contradict the long-held belief, she explained, and tell Japanese soldiers that it was okay to surrender after all. Soldiers would be more inclined to believe the orders had come in the wake of a shift at the top.

The others agreed that it was worth a shot, and Betty wrote the "official" order.

When creating propaganda aimed at the Japanese military, she could speak Japanese and read it well enough to translate captured letters and diaries, but she couldn't write it. Besides, Betty and her husband had learned Japanese in Hawaii, where it had evolved from the language spoken by the first Japanese farmers who came to the island. It was almost a different dialect.

The OSS had hired numerous *nisei*—second-generation Japanese-Americans—for MO to create propaganda as well as translate documents, but in most cases, English was their first language, and they had learned Japanese in school or at home in the US, not Japan. Their language skills and cultural knowledge wouldn't pass muster with native-born Japanese.

Back in Washington, Betty had corrected for this by sending her drafts to the MO office in New York, which used *issei*—native-born Japanese people living in the United States, mostly professors and POWs. But given the background of Emperor Hirohito—who was highly educated and well traveled—the document had to sound like he had actually written it.

Working with Betty was Bill Magistretti, a Navy lieutenant who worked in the Research & Analysis division of OSS before transferring into MO. He had been born in the US, but his family moved to Japan when he was young. He had gone to public school in Tokyo and later attended Waseda University in Tokyo, but even he wasn't equal to this task.

In an ideal world, Betty needed a Japanese prisoner of war who had been to college.

Even if she could find one, the prisoner had to be willing to help.

The British Army ran a POW camp nearby, and after pulling multiple strings, Betty and Magistretti headed off.

The officer who admitted them to the POW compound singled out a prisoner named Okamoto who was helping the Brits with their propaganda, who had told them "he would do anything to shorten the war."

When they entered Okamoto's room, the prisoner froze as his eyes locked on Magistretti, who did the same. They started up a rapid-fire Japanese dialogue that Betty couldn't follow. When he came up for air, Bill finally told Betty and the British officer that he and Okamoto had actually attended the same middle school in Tokyo.

Everyone was amazed at the grand coincidence, and Okamoto came on board to help his old schoolmate. He diligently worked on the order, and when he felt it would pass, he presented Bill and Betty with a final version, ready for the printer. They found an accommodating British officer in charge of an offset press, who happily printed off the fake orders.

A few days later, the forged orders were handed off to a Burmese OSS double agent, who then smuggled it into the knapsack of an enemy Japanese courier. What was left unsaid—and what everyone on the MO team knew—was that the only way to get the forged order into the knapsack was if the courier was dead. The Burmese agent was no stranger to this kind of job, and once the deed was completed, he stuck around to watch as a couple of Japanese soldiers found the courier, went through his knapsack as a matter of course, and found the fake orders.

Within days, Betty and the MO team received news that Japanese soldiers were surrendering in northern China. She was heartened by the news, but inwardly it bothered her. She loved her work, but of course there was a dark side. In fact, Betty, Jane, Zuzka, and Marlene would all struggle with being directly or indirectly responsible for causing death. After all, they were fighting a bloody, dirty, and uncertain war, and they fully realized the risk and consequences of their work. They tried to push it out of their minds, reminding themselves that every new leaflet and radio broadcast could save American lives and bring the war's end one day closer.

Betty's next project involved a batch of postcards that had been intercepted from Japanese soldiers stationed in Burma. The messages were pretty simple, mostly missives to family back home, containing nothing about the status of the war or morale since military censors had cleared them. The soldiers had used pencil instead of ink, so it was an easy job for Betty, Bill, and some of the *nisei* to erase a few words and insert new ones, like "The emperor has let us down, we are fighting with no food, no ammunition" or "I found a beautiful Burmese lady, Mom, and I won't be coming home."

"We wanted to show the total disillusionment of the Japanese soldiers in Burma," said Betty, "and we had a lot of fun thinking these things up." A courier smuggled the cards into the Japanese postal system.

Only three months after arriving in Delhi, Betty received some good news. She was appointed acting chief, Morale Operations of the China-Burma-India theater, though with a caveat: She'd hold the position only "until a suitable male replacement arrives from Washington." A few weeks later, Washington OSS decided to reorganize the MO bases and close the Delhi office, moving the entire staff to Calcutta to get a little closer to the field. Unfortunately, Betty's promotion was canceled in the process.

She took it in stride, taking some comfort in knowing that the new location would make her job easier: Printing facilities were already secured, and more translators were awaiting orders.

As the New Year approached and she prepared to head to Calcutta, Betty grew introspective. The last six months had been the most exciting of her entire life. But she couldn't ignore the fact that the world was still at war. "I suppose people were thinking it all over the world: Was this New Year 1945 to be the year of peace?"

Chapter 7

Marlene

In between war bond tours, Marlene continued to make movies, all solid fare that generated decent revenue at the box office, but just enough to pay her bills. "I only make action pictures these days," she said in an interview in 1942. "The public does not want polite drawing room comedies or too heavy drama now."

Marlene also threw herself into helping out at the Hollywood Canteen, which opened on October 3, 1942, in an abandoned nightclub. The venue was modeled after the successful Stage Door Canteen in Manhattan, which was a mix between a club and cafeteria that served as a stopping-off point for young soldiers heading off to war. Everything was free, and officers weren't allowed in unless they paid a hundred-dollar fee. The first night, three thousand patrons were expected, but over twelve thousand men showed up instead. Popular celebrities of the day, from Louis Armstrong to Laurel and Hardy, volunteered by dishing up plates of stew to the new recruits before entertaining them onstage. Duke Ellington and Xavier Cugat conducted the band while Eddie Cantor sang, and Marlene would often greet arriving servicemen at the door with Dinah Shore and Lana Turner.

Marlene loved the job, and between the cross-country bond tours, working at the canteen, and making an occasional movie, she was exhausted all the time, but here was a way that she could directly affect the lives of thousands of young men who were about to put their lives on the line. She had found her calling.

In addition to serving up meals on the cafeteria line, Marlene liked to clean pots and pans out back in the kitchen alongside Austrian-born actress Hedy Lamarr. Even when Marlene worked behind the scenes, she wore a dress that accentuated her every curve while plunging her hands into a sink full of soapy water.

"What is it with those *hausfraus*?" asked actress Bette Davis, who founded the Canteen along with actor John Garfield, and was in charge of scheduling entertainment out front for the troops. "Show them a kitchen and they're off like a horse to water! I need glamour out *here* for the boys, not in there with the pots!"

But Marlene wouldn't leave until the kitchen sparkled. "She'd be down on her hands and knees scrubbing the floor," Davis added. "She never worried about dishpan hands or scrubbing-floor knees. She really worked with elbow grease."

Marlene occasionally put down her sponge to take the stage out front to sing a few songs and play her violin, but the audience was really waiting for her to perform one act in particular: playing her musical saw. When the men saw her reach for her saw, the room exploded in cheers. And she knew how to play the room full of what were mostly teenagers: She'd take a seat at the center of the stage, where she'd suggestively position a saw between her legs, toss out some bawdy comment, and start to bow.

She freely admitted that her skills were rusty. "I dug up the saw from my basement and found that I am now terrible at playing it," she said. "But I figure the boys may enjoy me even more if I make a few mistakes." Her repertoire included everything from Schubert to "Pagan Love Song," and her audience loved her for it.

Once American soldiers started fighting in earnest, the inevitable casualties mounted, and many injured soldiers returned home for treatment. Marlene added military hospitals to her schedule, and in addition to entertaining soldiers on makeshift stages set up in hospital auditoriums, she also visited those who couldn't make it to the show in their hospital rooms. It's estimated that over 250,000 soldiers saw her perform during one stint up and down the West Coast.

* * *

On December 31, 1943, Marlene had just wrapped up production on her latest film, *Kismet*, and as she toasted the New Year, she was also fighting the symptoms of lead poisoning caused by painting her legs gold for the film.

"The dressing room reeked of toxic fumes, and the skin of her legs turned green under the thick coats of metal paint," said her daughter, Maria Riva. "Her stomach heaved and she was dizzy for days, on the brink of lead poisoning."

But the constant headache and numbness in her arms couldn't dampen her spirits because the USO had just announced that celebrities would finally be allowed to travel to Europe to entertain the troops. Like Betty and Zuzka, Marlene had spent months yearning to go overseas, and now she got her chance. She was grouped with Danny Thomas and a few other actors and singers who started to hone their act in a beat-up rehearsal room over Lindy's Restaurant in Times Square. Marlene sang, showed some leg, and played the violin and—of course—her musical saw.

Army censors had to green-light all the songs and skits, not for security reasons but because they didn't want the acts to offend the young green servicemen. As a result, the show was hokey as hell, but Marlene didn't care. Here, finally, was something she could do to help the soldiers she always called "her boys."

All of the entertainers on the tour were provided with a rank in case they were captured by the enemy; Marlene was granted the title of major, while Danny Thomas was relegated to a mere captain. After two months of rehearsals, the troupe tested out their act locally at war bond rallies and Army camps, and made their debut at Fort Meade in Maryland on March 20, 1944. Feedback was overwhelmingly positive, and two weeks later, they were told to be ready to ship overseas.

Marlene couldn't wait.

* * *

On tour, her outfits would be of paramount importance.

She packed the slinky sequin-studded gowns that had played such a crucial role on the war bond tour, but since all entertainers in the USO were automatically granted officer status, they were fitted for special uniforms made at Saks Fifth Avenue, one for summer and one for winter. Winter wear was known as "pinks and greens": a dark green wool coat and trousers and skirts of a lighter tan that looked pink if you squinted.

From the beginning, it was obvious that Marlene was privy to secrets and tidbits that other entertainers on the tour weren't. The military top brass were obviously grateful that Dietrich had taken such a strong stand for their side—and against the Nazis—and regularly rewarded her with perks and information.

Entertainers and military officers alike were never told of their destinations until they were well en route, so they brought uniforms suitable for both hot and cold climates. Maria Riva had by then become a singer who accompanied her mother with the USO, and she always suspected that Marlene had been alerted to her destinations in advance because she only brought one uniform with her: a summer uniform.

Marlene was limited to just fifty-five pounds of luggage for the entire trip, a huge change from the three dozen or more pieces of Louis Vuitton and Hermès suitcases and valises she usually toted around. So she whittled down her wardrobe to two floor-length gowns festooned with sequins ("guaranteed whistle bait," as *Vogue* put it); four short dresses, also with more sequins than fabric; gray flannel men's pants and a cashmere sweater; and, of course, her Army-issue uniform.

As they left for their first USO tour, they took off during a hailstorm.

It was Marlene's first-ever ride in an airplane. Movie studios took out insurance policies on her that forbade her from flying, so she had made all her previous Atlantic crossings by ship.

"When we landed there were no welcoming committees, nor did we expect any," she said. "All of our comings and goings had to be secret."

Marlene performed in her first USO show the day after landing in Morocco, and she was dropped in the deep end from the start. In the middle of the show, at the Algiers Opera House on April 11, 1944, the air raid sirens went off. She hurried off with other soldiers to the waterfront to watch Axis planes attack a convoy of supply ships right off the coast.

Marlene sang and performed in two shows a day, sometimes more. She and the others in her troupe were nothing but flexible. One day, they'd be in a glamorous opera house, while the next, they crammed onto the back of a truck and stood on empty ammunition crates.

"We do it just as Washington has approved it, not a line more or less," she said. "I sing 'See What the Boys in the Back Room Will Have' first because that's what they all want immediately. We do some skits. I play that musical saw." She also did a few mind-reading skits and some magic tricks, which she learned from Orson Welles, who years earlier sawed her in half onstage during a magic act. She finished up by singing a few hits from her movies, and she always ended her show with "Lili Marlene," which always brought the house down.

The smile she wore almost constantly while careening from military base to outpost to aircraft carrier was radically different from the seductive heavy-lidded half smile she had been paid hundreds of thousands of dollars to display on movie sets.

For one, it was *real*.

Besides, it was easier to smile now that she didn't have to tape her face.

On movie sets, she endured the no-tech facelifts that stretched her skin back for long hours on the set, first pulling back her cheeks and fixing them in place with gaffer tape borrowed from the young grips on set. She secured it all to the back of her neck, where one sultry hairstyle or another—requiring another couple of additional hours to arrange for the unsympathetic eye of the camera—hid the ends of the tape.

In the Army, Marlene was free. She didn't have to think about lighting, sets, staging, costume, makeup, hair, actors, or the director. She still wore a little makeup, though in the muffled light of blacked-out barracks and frequent dust storms and/or blizzards, her need was minimal. And she stopped shaving her eyebrows.

Life was simpler here, boiled down to the bare necessities, what-ever could fit in a small standard-issue military satchel. She gave two shows a day, traveling in a jeep on rough roads to get to the next post, eating cold C rations, with not enough fresh water to drink. Plus very little sleep.

But she absolutely loved it. She'd never felt as alive . . . or wanted. And she had only one thing to accomplish:

To cheer up her boys.

* * *

In June 1944, Marlene and her USO troupe arrived in Naples to en-tertain the troops. While her first show in Algiers was held in a big plush opera house, in Naples the USO performed in theaters that had been heavily damaged.

From there, they headed on to Sardinia, Corsica, and Anzio to do shows and visit field hospitals. Once Rome was liberated, a slew of shows followed. She celebrated briefly before checking herself into an Army hospital. She had pushed herself so hard that she came down with pneumonia.

"I've never been sick or missed a day of work in my life, so when I got a sore throat I kept right on doing my two shows a day," she said. "I took some pills and carried my sore throat from dispensary to dispensary. But I was finally ordered into a hospital, not as an entertainer but as a patient. When you work for the USO you're working for the Army. You can be court-martialed, so I obeyed."

When she recovered, she returned to the tour, and on June 6, 1944, she was in the middle of a performance in Anzio, Italy, when a soldier walked on to hand her a note.

She then announced D-Day to thousands of cheering GIs.

"You never heard such whistling and yelling in your life," she said.

*   *   *

Marlene never felt like she could do enough, so she cheerfully took on additional responsibilities like appearing on live radio broadcasts for the Armed Forces Network, something that many USO entertainers were starting to do.

At the time, radio programming was beginning to play a significant role in MO operations. The MO office in London was working closely with the British version of black radio known as Soldatensender West; "*Soldatensender*" was German for "Soldier's Station." The British produced the slanted news while the Americans provided the entertainment, broadcasting to civilians and troops throughout Germany. The premise of the operation was that the songs served as irresistible bait to reel in listeners so that they'd stick around long enough to listen to some propaganda-laced stories mixed in with news reports that were actually true.

The Nazis believed the station was run by an underground resistance movement hidden deep within Germany, and the station was extraordinarily popular with German soldiers since Nazi stations mostly played the latest speeches from Hitler and other Nazi officials, peppered with military marches and heavy Germanic classical music. Though German troops were threatened with execution for listening to Allied programs, they clearly preferred the MO alternative that played swing and other popular American music of the time. This fact was attested to by hundreds of prisoners of war who had been interrogated by Zuzka.

The American Broadcasting Station in Europe (ABSIE) was a collaboration between the BBC and the US Office of War Information, which was in charge of putting out white propaganda, the counterpart to MO's black propaganda. ABSIE was based in London, and its programs were primarily aimed at Europeans living under occupation, but also German civilians and military. It first went on the air in April 1944.

Marlene started to perform in a weekly program called *Marlene Sings to Her Homeland*. Whenever she landed in London between USO tours, she'd stop in and perform live or record several shows for the future. She told stories and sang a few songs, including old children's songs in German. She dedicated the song to the Allied soldiers "who were about to meet up with you boys and destroy the Reich."

"To the German officials, this radio program was very offensive and they were furious," Betty said years later after she had researched the role of women in the OSS and Morale Operations. "Marlene was anathema to a lot of the Germans in the same way an American would be to us who was working for the Germans or the Japanese. We would resent it terribly. German officials felt she was a traitor, betraying her country by singing these songs that upset many of the people listening."

One night, after she sang a few songs on a live broadcast, Marlene abruptly switched to German: "Boys! Don't sacrifice yourselves! The war is shit! Hitler is an idiot!" The radio announcer grabbed the mike, hissing that her audience consisted of American troops, but she was well aware that German civilians and soldiers listened to the show, too, and thought she'd kill two birds by buoying up the Allied spirit while depressing the morale of her fellow Germans, possibly making them more inclined to put down their rifles.

* * *

The tour was brutal, and danger lurked around every corner. But Marlene trusted that she was safe and that "her boys" would protect her. When it came to choosing locations for the USO tours, great care was taken. "After all, we were with the men and they weren't going to allow them to gather in large numbers where it would be easy for the enemy to get at them," she said. "Shows were held in closed theaters, on sand dunes, or from the backs of mobile trucks. And outdoor shows were never called off because of rain."

Marlene loved to perform out in the field, but what she came to enjoy more were the hospital shows and visits to patients afterward. Often three thousand wounded soldiers were crammed into a hastily set up Red Cross or Army hospital meant for one thousand. Lieutenant Russ Weiskircher of the 45th Infantry Division had been shot in the shoulder on an Anzio beachhead a month prior to one visit, and by the time Marlene showed up, he had recovered enough to guide her around.

"The show was presented to patients who could gather in the huge dining hall," he said. "Marlene sang, did magic tricks and told raunchy jokes, clad in a translucent, shimmering blue gown, slit to reveal those million-dollar legs. She hiked up her dress and paraded across the stage, tossing autographed blue garters to the audience. There was pandemonium, bedlam. Wheelchairs collided; crutches and canes became weapons as the men fought to capture a prize. The authorities had to stop the show to keep from adding to the casualty list," he said, only half joking.

After each hospital show, she headed directly for the wards, which reeked of decay and disinfectant. The doctors told her to douse herself with perfume before visiting patients. As one explained it to her, "Smelling perfume on a woman could make the difference between life and death."

According to Weiskircher, when she visited the patients, Marlene never stopped moving. "She sang, she joked, she gave autographs, she flirted," he said. "She visited every room except the quarantine ward. I struggled to keep up with her. She lived on cigarettes, coffee and martinis, worked 16-hour days every day, and was a hell of a trooper."

"One or two wanted to smoke, so I light cigarettes for them," she said. "They wanted their hands held, that's very important. In those wards you get a feeling of extraordinary confidence in everybody who's around. That's a marvelous feeling that you never get in civilian life no matter who you are."

Years after the war, Marlene would give an elegant, impassioned soliloquy to describe the months she spent alongside thousands of US troops. "There's something about an American soldier you can't explain," she said. "They're so grateful, so heartbreakingly grateful for anything. Bravery is simple when you're defending your own country, but these lonely men fighting on foreign soil accepted pain and mutilation as if they fought and fell defending their own soil. That made them the bravest of all."

Marlene and her troupe performed 150 shows over the course of ten weeks, for audiences ranging in size from 50 to 22,000. And she loved every minute of it.

When the tour wrapped up, she returned home only very reluctantly, and she made it very clear that she wanted to go back. "I'll go anywhere," she said.

But Bill Donovan had other plans for her.

* * *

For months, General Donovan had been receiving regular reports about Marlene's USO performances and hospital visits, and he was impressed. Marlene was different from the other entertainers. She wore her rank proudly, stopping at nothing to fight for her adopted country, and word soon spread throughout the OSS. "When she got as close as she could to the border, just to be there and help raise morale, well it impressed him terribly," said Betty.

After she returned to New York, Donovan paid her a visit, laying out his plans for a new clandestine program called the MUZAK Project that was gearing up in plain sight, right in Times Square.

He explained that he wanted to expand Soldatensender West, enhancing the musical selections by broadcasting popular American songs recorded by German singers in their native language. He figured this would help twist the heartstrings of German civilians and soldiers alike, bringing them one step closer to acknowledging the futility of continuing to fight an unwinnable war.

And in his opinion, there was no better performer to accomplish this than Marlene Dietrich. Donovan asked her to contribute a total of twelve songs to the project.

She quickly agreed.

Once she signed on, the project kicked into high gear.

First Donovan hired the J. Walter Thompson advertising agency to set up a dummy corporation to manage the project, choose the songs, audition singers, and book the studio and musicians.

The challenges were many; after all, everything needed to be done with the utmost secrecy, yet they had to hire top professional musicians—most of whom were union members living in New York—and native German-speaking singers without letting on about the true intention of the project. They also needed a top-notch lyricist fluent in English and German who could translate popular American songs like "This Can't Be Love" and "Oklahoma" from English into German and subtly turn these songs from upbeat to melancholy. Finally, with wartime shortages of acetate and vinyl, producing the actual records would also present some problems.

Bertolt Brecht, who had written the book for *The Threepenny Opera*, was originally hired as lyricist for the project, but he was soon dismissed because some in the OSS thought he was too avant-garde; plus, there were rumors that he was a Communist. So Lothar Metzl, who had built his reputation as a satirist in the nightclubs of Vienna and who had since joined the US Army, came on board to translate songs by George and Ira Gershwin, Cole Porter, and Irving Berlin, among others.

Noted German composer Kurt Weill, who wrote the music for *The Threepenny Opera*, orchestrated and arranged the OSS songs to suit the German mood and temperament, and his wife, singer Lotte Lenya, would record several songs on the project.

Many of the songs had no propaganda content but were intended solely to attract listeners to the news segments. Others had a nostalgic appeal designed to promote more weariness and defection. Still others were hard-hitting satirical songs attacking Nazi leaders, relating to the discomforts and disillusionment of war.

Marlene loved the project, and she was well aware there was a real risk in beaming her sonorous alto directly into her war-weary native country. Some Germans viewed her as a traitor. Indeed, in the thin-walled bombed-out tenements of Berlin and Dresden, neighbors who continued to toe the Nazi party line—despite mounting evidence that the German army was in retreat—were all too willing to turn in their neighbors to the local Gestapo.

But many Germans missed her voice; after all, she was the country's biggest export before the war. For many disgruntled Germans, hearing the sound of Marlene's voice—even at low volume on a transistor radio pressed against the head and with a blanket tightly tucked in to muffle any residual sounds—was worth the risk.

Besides, there was no other American singer who had the essential ingredient: "I am German and I understand the Germans," she affirmed.

Just like Jane, who had spent years alongside the Japanese, she knew best how to hurt them, and what would push their buttons.

Marlene's friend Ernest Hemingway, who called her "the Kraut," agreed. "Even if she had nothing else but her voice, she could break hearts with it," he said.

And if she couldn't be with her boys in person, at least here was something she could do to help them right now.

Chapter 8

Jane

When Jane and Cynthia sailed into New York Harbor aboard the *Gripsholm* on August 23, 1942, Jane was overjoyed to see her husband greet the ship, along with her mother, who had traveled from Sioux City. Henri felt bad about suddenly leaving his family in Rio and decided to make it up to them by meeting the ship and spending a few days in New York to help get them settled into a hotel for a brief stay.

After the trauma of their six-month confinement and the uncertainty of their future together during wartime, Jane was thrilled to spend any amount of time with her husband, especially since Henri had been promoted to fleet commander shortly after arriving back in the States with the expectation that he would spend the duration of the war at sea. Jane knew that future visits would be few and far between.

However, Henri was transferred to a position that required him to be based in Washington, DC, not at sea, which surprised them both, so Jane set about finding a place for them to live near the nation's capital. Life in Washington was bustling, with so many people arriving each day, all looking for a job and a place to live. It quickly became very expensive to live in the city, as food prices increased by a third and rents increased by as much as 300 percent in just one year.

Despite the wartime housing shortage, she found a small house on Brandywine Street on the edge of Rock Creek Park. After dealing with the movers, arranging furniture, and getting oriented in her new neighborhood, she found herself—for the first time in years— with no idea what to do.

After all, it was wartime, and her previous activities—taking classes, entertaining women with luncheon and bridge games, and immersing herself in a foreign culture—paled in importance. Henri's schedule was understandably packed, his responsibilities so encompassing that twelve-hour workdays were the rule; it was not unusual for him to nod off at the dinner table.

As the wife of a Navy officer, Jane had an easier life than most; she didn't have to worry about money, and she could afford to hire a woman to care for the house and for Cynthia. But many store shelves were empty, and butter and coffee were in especially short supply by the beginning of 1943. Meat was a rare luxury, and gasoline was rationed to three gallons a week. The list of unavailable foods and products would grow longer as the war dragged on—the three pairs of shoes allotted annually to each American was soon reduced to two—but Jane's previous experience navigating the black markets in Tokyo came in handy as they started to pop up throughout Washington.

In the nation's capital, residents of the city became accustomed to constantly feeling like they were under imminent attack—from Germany, or Japan, or both. Indeed, air raid sirens went off at all hours for practice drills, with people heading for basements and ducking under the nearest tree with only a few seconds' notice.

But even in wartime Washington, there was a cultured class of Ladies Who Lunch who continued on with their normal schedules in the early years of the war amid nightly blackouts, air raid sirens, and limited gas and food supplies. After a year of not working, Jane was restless. She put together a series of lectures and classes on Japanese culture and *ikebana*—the art of Japanese flower arranging— and contacted local women's groups and cultural clubs to offer her services. While most Americans considered the Japanese a detested enemy, Jane thought that a more cultured and educated group of ladies—who, like her, had perhaps spent time in the Far East before the war—might appreciate learning more about Japanese tradition. And by focusing on the positive aspects of the culture, perhaps Jane could forget that Japan essentially held her and her family hostage in Tokyo for more than six months.

The League of Women Voters and numerous other organizations happily booked Jane at a rate of $150 to $200 an hour, an inordinate sum at the time. She regularly traveled up and down the Eastern Seaboard to give her lectures.

Despite the money, Jane soon became frustrated focusing on the lighter side of Japanese culture while the war intensified. And as the wife of a career military officer, she also clearly had no patience for those who whined about shortages of everything from sugar to shoes. "We are soft here—we haven't begun to feel the war yet," she told a women's group in Fairfield, Connecticut, in April 1943. "And many people still don't know that they have more to eat than our men out there doing the fighting. But you can't win a war without rationing; before this war is over, none of us will have enough to eat. Our men, they are the ones who must get everything. We don't count—we aren't important any more."

However, pointing out the weaknesses of civilians was starting to hit home for her in a different way. It seemed like every adult in Washington but her was working six days a week—five days a week was considered to be part-time—to help bring a quicker end to the war. Jane yearned to participate more actively in the war effort. Besides, by late 1943, her bookings had started to drop off as even the Ladies Who Lunch realized that taking classes in Japanese flower arranging did little to enhance their standing in wartime Washington. By then, most were busy tending their victory gardens, donating their scrap metal to the government, and spending their money buying war bonds, not on frivolous lectures and workshops about the enemy.

By the end of 1943, Jane had had enough. As the war intensified and Wild Bill Donovan started to ramp up staffing at all departments of the OSS, he was keeping his eyes peeled for civilians and military personnel who knew the Japanese language. When Donovan got wind of the wife of a former naval attaché who was extremely well-versed in Asian culture—and fluent in Japanese to boot—he put her in his crosshairs.

They arranged a meeting, and he quickly offered Jane a job at Morale Operations. When Henri found out, he tried to dissuade his wife from taking the job. As a career military man trained to do everything by the book, he believed the OSS was populated with spies and ne'er-do-wells who cut corners and lacked discipline. Jane patiently listened to her husband's concerns, and then dismissed them. After all, joining the OSS was a way she could contribute to the war effort by calling upon her very specific and rare skills.

* * *

Jane reported to the Morale Operations office on February 7, 1944. Her title was project specialist and administrative assistant to the head of the Japan desk, and she was hired on a part-time basis of five days a week at an annual salary of $2166.

She stood out at the typically lax MO office. As the daughter of an army officer *and* the wife of a naval attaché, she was a bit of an anomaly compared with the ragtag group of civilian recruits. For one, she always signed her documents as "J. S-H."—short for Jane Smith-Hutton—and she took her job deadly seriously.

She and Betty worked on a number of projects together, and Betty was amused by the difference between them. "She added a bit of spit and polish, and also order, to an otherwise laid back group of ex-newspaper reporters, artists, cartoonists and radio announcers," Betty said years later.

Like the other MO staff in the Far East office, Jane attended mandatory training sessions in Japanese culture and language when she first started her job, but it didn't take long for her to grasp that she knew far more than the instructors. Since Jane had lived in Tokyo and had studied the Japanese language there, she had learned how to speak and write the enemy's language, not the more formal kind learned through textbooks or filtered through one or more generations in Hawaii.

Her instructors were impressed, and in short order Jane was teaching several classes—alongside future famed anthropologist Margaret Mead, another OSS instructor—and vetting propaganda slated for distribution. She was also asked to review drafts of leaflets and other materials slated for distribution, and she often found errors in the style and language, telling the instructor that if a faulty leaflet was distributed, the Japanese would immediately know it was a fake, which would likely result in Allied lives lost.

One of her first responsibilities was to serve as a clearinghouse for all the information that flooded the office each day from more than thirty spies working all over the Far East. She had to decide if the tips and leads were worth passing on to those who could make the most use of them, or if she should discard them instead. As a result, Jane quickly learned an important lesson about working in wartime that the other OSS women also absorbed early on. Whenever she came up with an idea for a leaflet or had feedback on a radio script, she had initially asked higher-ups for permission to proceed, but a response often arrived either much later or not at all, since everyone was too busy with their own projects. She was lucky to get a quick glance and a wave to say *It's fine*. After all, they trusted her.

Eventually she stopped asking, and no one complained. In fact, her coworkers and supervisors regularly complimented her on her work.

A few months later, she shifted to working full-time with a corresponding bump in pay to $2600 a year.

* * *

One job that Jane took on involved purchasing Japanese books, periodicals, and newspapers. They would help her to educate personnel in her lectures and also keep her up-to-date on any news or trends that didn't arrive via the standard OSS channels. But the job was also a risky one. At the time, Americans' suspicions toward anything Japanese or German were running high. Both the federal government and local law enforcement officials instructed civilians to report anyone doing anything that looked like it might benefit the Germans or Japanese.

Since many OSS employees fluent in Japanese had long ago been sent overseas, finding people stateside who could read, write, and speak the language—and know which publications to buy— were few and far between. Jane appreciated any opportunity to take a break from the office, and she regularly traveled outside Washington to locate and buy Japanese books, newspapers, and magazines. It was a delicate balancing act; she often had to simultaneously charm a naturally suspicious store clerk while looking over her shoulder to see if anyone—an American *or* Japanese spy—was following her. A precarious task to be sure. Soon employees from other OSS departments were asking her to buy books and newspapers for them, too.

Jane traveled to New York on several occasions for buying expeditions. But soon buying *any* publications became an operation in frustration. Not only did Japanese-language publications become scarce as the war dragged on and the supply chain ground to a halt, but newspapers and magazines that made it out of Japan were too out-of-date to provide usable information or a sample that MO's typesetters and printers could mimic in terms of paper, ink, and typeface. Jane started to place orders with secondhand bookstores, but they faced the same issues she did. In July 1944, Jane placed an order for a 1935 book on Japanese Buddhism, the latest edition of *Who's Who in Japan, When Japan Goes to War,* and *Militarism and Fascism in Japan.* The total cost was about one hundred dollars—or more than two weeks of her salary—so she filed a requisition order and then waited.

After a month, she decided to front the money out of her own pocket to buy the books she needed. But along with the unpredict-ability of being able to locate and then purchase a particular book within a certain time frame, Jane was far more frustrated at the roadblocks that her male higher-ups placed in front of her. After all, she was still at the lowest rung of the OSS pay scale even though she was far more skilled—and regularly completed more projects—than her male counterparts.

Though the OSS employed over four thousand women—out of a total of 21,640 employees—many career military officers were not happy about their female coworkers and regularly took their wrath out on female staffers, particularly highly intelligent women like Jane. MO and the OSS as a whole tended to be a lot more freewheel-ing than the stiff military establishment, where protocol and tradi-tion ruled, and many longtime officers obviously resented having to interact with civilians who lacked respect for military customs.

As a result, Jane's requests were frequently shot down. She re-quested a translation of a 1936 biography of the pioneer patriots of East Asia, which would require pulling some of the *nisei* and *issei* employees away from their work. Indeed, translating a thousand pages of text *was* a lot of work, and her superior Captain Randall Clark turned down her request but then asked her to provide him with a report about Allied intelligence in Germany, which, of course, wasn't her beat. Besides, she couldn't spare the time.

But she felt like she couldn't say no, so she did the best she could and focused on the things she could control . . .

. . . like her Rumor Mill sessions. Since she was the primary point of contact for thirty spies reporting in from all over the world, Jane kept up-to-date on intelligence and military developments that could be used to create new pieces of propaganda. She decided to hold weekly meetings where she and her coworkers could toss ideas around based on the reports that had come into the office during the previous week. The aim was to come up with the most hurtful—but still plausible—rumors that they could pass on to OSS outposts throughout the Far East, which could then be spread among the Japanese.

In the official OSS *Morale Operations Field Manual*, spreading rumors was held in high regard. "A good rumor is one which will spread widely in a form close to that of the original story," which was why receiving raw intelligence from agents in the field was so important. And rumors kicked into high gear once the Axis began to falter in the war, because according to the manual, "subversive rumors against the enemy are used to exploit the fear and anxiety of those who have begun to lose confidence in military success."

Primary rumor targets included "groups that have become fearful and anxious about their personal well-being . . . who are suspicious of or hate other groups or leaders . . . and whose monotonous, humdrum lives make them particularly susceptible to fantasy: for example, men in army camps."

Coming up with rumors was great fun, and often the highlight of the week for Jane and her coworkers. MO staffers both stateside and overseas looked forward to the fruits of her weekly Rumor Mill sessions, where they would compete to come up with the most outrageous—but still believable—rumors.

For instance, Jane reported, "to create the impression that hostile natives are putting ground glass into food supplied by the Japanese," she suggested a rumor "using the names of two most recently captured POWs or identified corpses and say they died in the hospital last week from poisoning by ground glass. To cover up the real cause of death they have been reported as 'missing in action.'"

She came up with another example, again using the names of two most recently captured POWs or identified corpses: "Two men died after a blood transfusion in which the new Japanese synthetic blood made from seaweed derivative was used. First they fell into a coma, then they writhed and frothed at the mouth. Finally they died."

Rumors could be developed into pamphlets and incorporated into radio broadcasts and underground newspapers. But they could also be disseminated the old-fashioned way: through word of mouth. "The rumors can be smuggled in through servants, tradesmen, and written up for insertion and foodstuffs, or left around in places where Japanese soldiers come, or stuck up in trees on the trails," Jane wrote in a report disseminated throughout the MO office in Washington. "Most importantly, the rumor should be specific, and preferably backed up by a half-truth."

Though rumors were the basis of the field manual, military officers didn't hesitate to show their displeasure at these less conventional methods. In a letter to Jane, Major William E. Boldt, one of her superiors in the Washington MO office, changed the rules in the middle of the game. "The word 'rumor' is negative," he wrote in a memo. "It makes the man who relays it doubt its value, as well as the contents . . . and he is liable to think it unimportant. So we have stopped talking about rumors . . . our communications to the field now talk about INFORMATION MATERIAL . . . and each rumor is called 'Info.'"

When Jane read the memo, she probably reacted the same way Betty and Zuzka did when called onto the carpet by a clueless officer: She ignored it, business as usual, with Donovan's words echoing in her head:

"If you think it will work, go ahead."

* * *

Betty often attended Jane's Rumor Mill sessions, and soon they began to work together on ideas for leaflets and rumors as well as songs. Since many Japanese soldiers were illiterate, MO staffers always liked to err on the side of simplicity, and often looked to cartoons and even songs to convey a particular message. In June 1944, Betty and Jane collaborated on a takeoff of "The Bugle Call to Charge," a popular Japanese song written from the viewpoint of a young soldier who died in battle. The song was designed to inspire other soldiers to continue fighting and believe in victory, but Jane and Betty's version twisted the meaning.

After victory we shall meet again
Those were your words to me.
I then believed in Victory
And in the world to be.

Nothing remains but tatters.
A funeral dirge is all we hear
We feel we fight in vain.

Not very inspirational. Betty crafted a brief background to appear alongside the lyrics. "Only the soldiers dying on the battlefields know the meaning of the song on the left, written by Private Toshio Yamamoto, a young college student, just before he died in a Burma jungle," she wrote. "This pamphlet is produced by the Nihon Heiwa Domei, a peace organization of Japanese who are fighting for the welfare of a greater Japan."

She also came up with an idea for a painting for the cover of the leaflet: a Japanese soldier wrapped in a torn flag, covered in blood against a background of burned-out fields and buildings.

The two women enjoyed working together on new ideas for rumors and other propaganda, but their collaborations ended when Betty's long-awaited overseas transfer came in July 1944.

Jane would miss her friend, because collaborating with her was one of the few ways she could be sure to make time to work on her own projects. With Betty gone, Jane was just too busy. She spent the bulk of her working hours reading, analyzing, and steering documents, reports, and intelligence to other staff in the field and in Washington, which didn't leave time to conjure up her own propaganda. This undoubtedly intensified her frustration at the limitations of her job pay grade and title; after all, working six full days a week, and sometimes more, she was still only making fifty bucks a week . . . before taxes.

After twenty-two months living and working in Washington, Henri was finally ordered to sea duty as the commander of Destroyer

Squadron 15 in the Atlantic fleet in October 1944, where he'd help escort convoys to and from the Mediterranean theater, and where lurking enemy submarines were never far away. After he left, Jane threw herself into her work in an attempt to not think about the danger he faced.

She decided that it was high time that she be promoted; after all, like Betty and Zuzka, she was often doing twice the work of her male colleagues, and getting paid significantly less. She applied for an up-grade from project specialist CAF-7, which paid $2600, to project specialist CAF-9, with a salary of $3200. It wasn't much, but it would provide confirmation that what she was doing was valuable.

The required written recommendations she collected from co-workers were glowing:

"She holds a very responsible position and is one of the most valuable of our staff members. The requested increase in salary is well-deserved."

"She is one of the most well-informed individuals on conditions in Japan who we have on our staff."

But her request for a promotion was turned down. The excuse was that she lacked sufficient work experience.

Jane must have raised enough of a stink at her rejection that Edna F. Stonesifer, acting chief of the OSS employment division, wrote a letter asking the commission to reconsider their decision. "It is felt that she warrants the Commission's approval due to her unique qualifications. [She is] highly skilled in handling the intricate prob-lems involved . . . and she is the best available qualified candidate for the position."

Ten days later, the request was again rejected. Jane was outraged. She applied one more time, and whether it was due to her stubborn-ness or perhaps some money being reallocated from one budget to another, on January 1, 1945, she was promoted to the level of project specialist CAF-9 at a new yearly salary of $3200 plus overtime, though she kept the same title of assistant to the head of the Japan desk.

Jane was pleased, but perturbed that it took several tries to get promoted. Job descriptions at MO were very fluid due to the constant flow of new projects and tasks that staffers encountered on a daily basis. Besides, everybody was so flat out with work that nobody really noticed—or cared—what your title was, or if you just gave yourself a new one.

So after she was promoted, Jane simply began to refer to herself as "Chief, Japan MO."

After all, that's what black propaganda was—telling believable lies—and Jane was a very good student.

ACT THREE

BELIEVABLE
LIES

Chapter 9

Zuzka

The first Sauerkraut mission proved to be so successful that more were planned. Zuzka became the go-to person for POW interrogations, and she made regular trips to Caserta every few weeks to interview a fresh batch of POWs.

Her interrogations served double duty, for military intelligence as well as for her own MO purposes. Not only could she screen for POWs who would be effective for the operation, but she could also ask them about German military operations and the strengths—and weaknesses—of their units. Zuzka would then submit reports to the US Army to help in planning strategy and future missions.

And sometimes they'd say something that would spark an idea for a piece of propaganda.

She quickly discovered that being a woman *and* a foreigner worked in her favor: For one, her accent and fluent German often caught POWs off guard since they were unsure which side she was on. The men were also thrown by the appearance of the petite, pretty blond woman who was interrogating them, as opposed to a couple of gruff, burly soldiers who liked to play good cop, bad cop.

Zuzka did her best to always keep them guessing: Was she a fellow POW who had turned for the Allies? Or maybe some Yank officer's girl on the side? The more sharp-eyed POWs might have noticed the lack of stripes on her arm—she remained a private despite possessing skills that most officers lacked—but in any event, they probably relaxed more with Zuzka than they would have with any male interrogator.

After the first Sauerkraut operation, Zuzka's grilling sessions fell into an easy pattern. She'd start by asking the POW a few direct questions, and once she got a sense of the person beneath the war-torn soldier—either dyed-in-the-wool Nazi or young and scared boy, still in his teens—she'd transform. With the trembling little boys, she'd morph into a caring maternal figure. On the other side of the spectrum, she'd play coy with an imperceptible touch of the flirt. And in most cases, the prisoners would flirt right back.

She mostly just let the prisoners talk, though, listening to how they felt about the current state of the war and what they thought would happen in the near and distant future. If she was lucky, they'd spill a few juicy details about their individual units and their locations, and their present strengths and weaknesses. Afterward, she'd type up an intelligence report providing details about troop movements, future military plans, and the like.

Then she'd roll the facts around in her mind and cook up a few ways to use them to create her own black propaganda.

* * *

In September 1944, Zuzka was back in Caserta, making her way through the latest batch of POWs. She was exhausted by the long drive to the POW camp the night before, but motored through the interrogations.

On to the next one. The POW's head snapped up when Zuzka flung back the flap and walked into the tent. His eyes widened as they ran the length of her body. She waited. As the only woman among twenty-three men in the MO office—and surrounded by hundreds more in the course of a normal day—she was used to this. She waited a few seconds for his eyes to return to hers.

Jane studied Japanese watercolor painting while she was in Tokyo. "The way in which different shades are applied with one stroke of the brush is truly fascinating," she told the *Tokyo Times* in 1940.

Jane celebrates her daughter Cynthia's seventh birthday in Tokyo, April 1941. They would be taken captive at the US embassy in Tokyo later that year.

Jane Smith-Hutton in 1943, shortly before she began work at the OSS.

Betty and two coworkers at the Morale Operations print shop in Kunming, China, in 1945.

Zuzka invented a leaflet for the "League of Lonely War Women" that falsely told war-weary German soldiers that women all over Germany "ARE WAITING FOR YOU."

Sommer 1944.

Lieber Frontsoldat!

Wann kommst Du wieder auf Urlaub?

Wann wirst Du Deine harten Soldatenpflichten wieder einmal vergessen können, wenigstens für ein paar Tage voll Freude, Glück und Liebe? Wir in der Heimat wissen von Deinem heldenhaften Kampf, wir verstehen aber, dass auch der Tapferste einmal müde wird und ein so ftes Kissen, Zärtlichkeit und gesundes Vergnügen braucht.

WIR WARTEN AUF DICH:

auf Dich, der in einer fremden Stadt allein seinen Urlaub verbringen muss; auf Dich, dem der Krieg sein Heim genommen hat; auf Dich, der ohne Frau, Braut oder Flirt in der Welt steht.

WIR WARTEN AUF DICH:

schneide unser Abzeichen aus diesem Briefe aus. In jedem Kaffee, in jeder Bar in der Nähe eines Bahnhofs, lehne es sichtbar an Dein Glas; gar bald wird sich ein Mitglied unseres V.E.K. Deiner annehmen, und Deine Fronträume und die Sehnsucht einsamer Nächte werden Erfüllung finden... Wir wollen Dich, nicht Dein Geld, darum lass Dir stets unsere Mitgliedskarte vorher zeigen. Mitglieder gibt es überall, da wir deutsche Frauen unsere Pflichten zur Heimat und ihren Verteidigern verstanden haben.

Natürlich sind wir auch selbstsüchtig — jahrelang von unseren Männern getrennt, mit all den Fremden um uns herum, möchten wir wieder einmal einen richtigen deutschen Jungen an's Herz drücken. Nur keine Hemmungen: Deine Frau, Schwester oder Geliebte ist auch eine der unseren.

V·E·K·

Wir denken an Dich und auch an Deutschlands Zukunft. Was rastet — rostet...

VEREIN EINSAMER KRIEGERFRAUEN

(Below) Zuzka and cartoonist Saul Steinberg came up with the idea for toilet paper with Hitler's face on it. *Diese Seite Benützen* is German for "Use This Side."

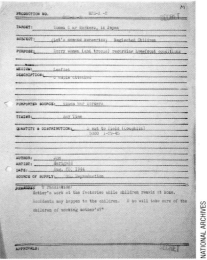

(Left) Jane produced a leaflet that underscored the danger that children faced while unsupervised at home because their mothers were working in factories to support the war effort. *(Right)* The work order for "Let's Demand Nurseries."

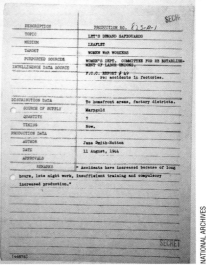

(Left) Jane created leaflets to spread the word about the unsafe conditions women faced working in factories. *(Right)* The work order for "Let's Demand Safeguards."

Zuzka and Saul Steinberg in the Morale Operations office in Rome in 1944.

The outside of the OSS office in Rome in the Piazza Don Minzoni.

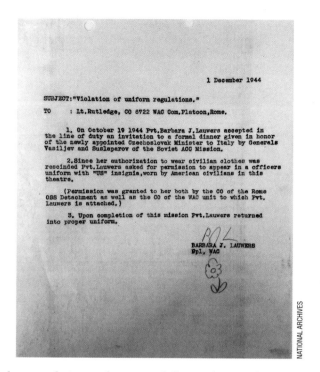

1 December 1944

SUBJECT: "Violation of uniform regulations."

TO   : Lt.Rutledge, CO 6722 WAC Com.Platoon,Rome.

1. On October 19 1944 Pvt.Barbara J.Lauwers accepted in the line of duty an invitation to a formal dinner given in honor of the newly appointed Czechoslovak Minister to Italy by Generals Vasiljev and Suslaparov of the Soviet ACC Mission.

2. Since her authorization to wear civilian clothes was rescinded Pvt.Lauwers asked for permission to appear in a officers uniform with "US" insignia,worn by American civilians in this theatre.

(Permission was granted to her both by the CO of the Rome OSS Detachment as well as the CO of the WAC unit to which Pvt. Lauwers is attached.)

3. Upon completion of this mission Pvt.Lauwers returned into proper uniform.

BARBARA J. LAUWERS
Cpl, WAC

NATIONAL ARCHIVES

Due to her translation and writing skills, Zuzka was frequently invited to military functions, despite her holding the lowly rank of private. She donned an officer's uniform for a special function and was cited for violations. She smoothed over the conflict, signing her report with a flower.

NATIONAL ARCHIVES

In recognition of her work on the Sauerkraut operation, resulting in six hundred Czechs and Slovaks surrendering to the Allies, Zuzka was awarded the Bronze Star on April 6, 1945.

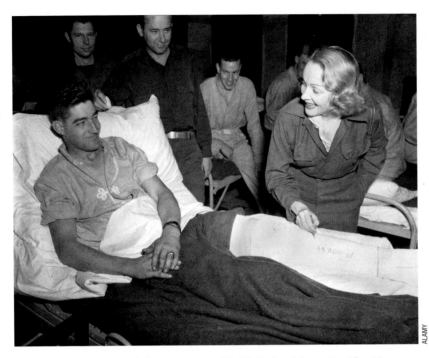

Marlene signs a leg cast belonging to Earl E. McFarland from Cavider, Texas, at a hospital in Belgium.

Marlene posing for a photo with General George Patton in 1944. "It'll do the soldiers good to know that you're at the front," he told her before her second USO tour. "They'll tell themselves the situation can't be so bad if [you're] there. If we were all going to be mowed down here, the old man certainly wouldn't expose her to such danger."

Dietrich hangs out with a group of WACs at an Army base somewhere in France in 1945.

On her USO tours, Marlene knew "her boys" loved when she dressed up in feather boas and skintight gowns, but she prepared for the often-biting cold by donning long underwear under her glamorous outfits and switching out Army-issue boots for stilettos at the very last minute.

Marlene frequently traveled with the USO to the front to entertain US troops.

A few years after the war, music impresario Mitch Miller convinced Marlene to re-record the OSS songs that were broadcast into Germany over the last year of the war. *Marlene Dietrich Overseas* came out in 1952 and was an immediate hit. Songs included "Miss Otis Regrets," "Taking a Chance on Love," and, of course, "Lili Marlene."

This one was young, just a scared boy. She offered him a cigarette—in the time that she'd been interrogating POWs, she discovered that their answers were much more forthcoming when she proffered the Camels, Marlboros, or the favored Lucky Strikes that came in her weekly GI ration. She tried a British brand once, but the POW frowned and pressed his lips tightly together at the clearly inferior smokes. Everyone at the post smoked but her, so her stockpile grew each week and came in handy when she had to bum rides with officers or wanted to trade them for some of that chocolate-hazelnut *pasta gianduja* that she loved.

Whenever a prisoner clammed up, she'd take the pack from her pocket and wave it in front of his face. If he still resisted, she'd light up one for herself and blow the smoke rings right into his face, though she mostly used it as a prop, only pretending to take a puff every now and then.

This time the boy's eyes softened. She held out her standard-issue Zippo lighter, and he cupped his hands around the end of the cigarette, despite the fact that there was little risk of a breeze passing through the musty tent walls.

Here was a connection, she thought. She waited for the first rush of nicotine to hit his brain, requested name-rank-and-serial, and then began.

"So," she said, a bit breathily, "where are you from?"

Her hard-line questions and his responses quickly morphed into small talk. As she'd suspected when she first saw him, he was a scared German farm boy drafted against his will who just wanted the war to be over. There was no danger here and no intelligence to be gathered from this low-rank recruit. Now it was time for some MO research.

Zuzka usually liked to pace back and forth in the beginning of an interrogation, to make it clear who was in charge, but this time she dragged a stool over and sat down to face the young man head-on.

"What bothers you most when you get news from home?" she asked, her voice gentler than before. "Is it the air raids, lack of food, what?"

"My woman." His voice was a whisper.

"What about her?"

He glanced at the dirt floor. "She might be screwing another guy."

Zuzka's eyes widened. She'd been trying to come up with some angles for leaflets aimed at the German civilian population.

"Go on," she said, and all at once, the boy poured his fears out.

"I've been gone from home so long, the Nazi officers in my hometown can easily buy my girlfriend food and clothes from Paris, and I haven't received a letter from her in months." An idea crystallized in Zuzka's mind, but the boy looked so miserable that she tamped her excitement down.

When he finished, she gave him an extra cigarette as a reward. He looked so startled by this unexpected kindness that he blinked back tears.

"*Danke,*" he said.

"*Bitte.*" She stood up to leave.

She launched the League of Lonely War Women the next day when she returned to Rome.

Dear Front Soldier,

When will you come back on leave?

When will you be able again to forget the hard duties of a soldier and exchange them for a few days of joy, happiness and love? Back at home we know of your heroic struggle; however, we do understand that even the bravest gets tired and that he needs a soft pillow, tenderness and healthy pleasure.

WE ARE WAITING FOR YOU

For you who have been compelled to spend your leave in a foreign town; we are waiting for you whom the war has robbed of his home, waiting for you who stands alone in the world without a wife, without a fiancée, without a flirt.

WE ARE WAITING FOR YOU

Cut out our badge on this letter. Display it visibly on your

glass in every tea room, in every bar which is in the vicinity of
a railway station; soon a member of our League of Lonely War
Women will take charge of you, and the dreams you dreamt
in the front line and the longings of lonely nights will find
fulfillment. It is you we want, not your money. Therefore ask for
our membership card at once. There are members everywhere,
since we German women understand our duties towards our
country and towards those who defend it.

Naturally, we are not unselfish—for years and years we have
been separated from our menfolk, surrounded by all these
foreigners; naturally we long to have again a real German boy,
to press him to our bosom. Don't be shy; your wife, your sister,
or your sweetheart is also one of us.

We think of you but we also think of the future of our
country. He who rests, rusts.

League of Lonely War Women

Zuzka wrote and proofed the letter in one day, and thousands of
leaflets were printed within the week. The leaflet included a small
drawing of two intertwined hearts, one with a key, the other with a
keyhole, making the sexual implications hard to miss. A soldier was
instructed to attach "the badge" to his uniform or set it on a table in
front of him, and soon love-starved women in small towns all over
Germany would be competing for the chance to take him home,
give him a good meal, and take him to bed.

Germany's birth rate had understandably plummeted during
the war, threatening Hitler's dream of filling the country—and indeed, the whole of Europe—with pure-blooded Aryan babies. And
between the lines, in Zuzka's words: "We not only want him to feel
good, we also want to get pregnant again and have babies in case our
own men don't come home."

A newly screened group of sixteen POWs—all personally interrogated by Zuzka—smuggled the propaganda into German-occupied

parts of Italy, dropping them near military bases, in bars, restaurants, and hotels, and in public squares before returning to safety a few days later.

It didn't take long for reports to filter back about German soldiers wandering through small towns and villages, the interlocked hearts pinned to their uniform, waiting for a woman—*any* woman—to show them her membership card and bring them home for a hot meal, uninterrupted sleep in a real bed, and, of course, a night of unbridled passion. But there was a flip side: Rather than being enticed by the prospect of experiencing the League's pleasures for himself, many a soldier angrily crumpled up the paper as it fed his fears of his own woman taking in one of his own comrades for the night . . . or longer.

There are no details about how German women reacted to the bedraggled, gaunt, lice-infested soldiers who followed them all over town like lovesick puppies, but it's likely that many of them wrote off the troops' delusions as proof that the war had gone on too long, which handily accomplished the other MO goal of demoralizing civilian populations as well.

Several newspapers back in the United States even took the bait, including *The Washington Post*, which ran a story about the League, with the headline "Free Love Offered to Nazis on Furlough." When a non-MO colleague in the Rome office read the story and remarked to Zuzka, "Can you believe these Germans?" she promptly replied, "Would you care to see the blueprint?"

* * *

Zuzka, of course, loved her job, and for the most part, her male colleagues respected her ideas and didn't talk down to her or denigrate her ideas just because she was a woman.

But as Jane had discovered, the US military wasn't as progressive. Military top brass had strict protocol to follow when granting promotions and increased pay, and while they often loosened the reins for men, the lack of advancement was a continuing thorn in the sides of Zuzka and the other women in MO who were performing comparable work to men, and typically doing more of it. Memos in the personnel files for Zuzka show numerous occasions where her male coworkers requested that her pay grade and rank be raised.

"Pvt. Lauwers is constantly being assigned to do business with ranking officers. In just one day she carried on transactions with a British captain, a major, and two other captains. She has been in consultations with ministers of state from Russia and Czechoslovakia, and it is a source of embarrassment to her and those she meets that she holds the lowest rank in the U.S. Army," read one impassioned missive.

But higher-ups repeatedly turned them down, amounting to a kind of morale operation directly aimed at their own female staff. *Don't get used to this*, the constant stream of rejections implied, *because when the war is over, you'll all go back to being wives and mothers.*

Indeed, one male personnel director justified his rejection of Zuzka by writing, "She is very highly emotional and lacks judgment and discretion," which was ironic since he had never met her.

For Zuzka, because she was an enlisted member of MO, the fact that she was a private—the lowest rank in the military—proved to be a never-ending source of aggravation as she regularly performed work that was more in line with an officer's duties.

Her lack of rank created all sorts of issues. While she did receive permission to wear an officer's uniform to interrogate the POWs, she had to revert to the rank of private the rest of the time. In the fall of 1944, she traveled to Florence with her MO colleague Captain Joseph Kolisch. At one point, Kolisch realized that a private would never be taken seriously by the civilians and other military personnel they'd encounter on their mission, so he hastily sewed a higher rank onto her sleeve.

On another occasion, she was asked to a formal dinner in Rome to honor the recent appointment of the new Czech ambassador to Italy, and except for Zuzka, only officers were invited. Since the NATO rules of war prevented military personnel from appearing in civilian clothes, Zuzka had to request special permission to wear an officer's uniform to the event. She attended the dinner, and later headed back to the barracks where she was staying with other WACs. Already suspicious of her "Damn Foreigner" accent and jealous of her work and travels, her dormmates—who invariably held higher rank—complained when she failed to remove her insignia and reported her for impersonating an officer.

"The other girls who worked in regular non-OSS Army units looked at us less than warmly since they already thought that we had too many privileges," she said. But the other female officers also weren't thrilled when Zuzka had to subvert the rules: "'You're not an officer, how dare you do that?'"

But skirting strict military rule was what MO—and the OSS—was all about, and necessary in order to get any work done. Zuzka also felt that she was caught in a no-man's-land between the Army and the OSS. She was particularly rankled that on her regular forays to interrogate POWs, her driver was an Army major who camped out in the jeep reading a comic book while she risked her life inside the interrogation tent.

Zuzka had long accepted that as a woman and a foreigner, her advancement in rank would be limited, and she always handled it with grace and aplomb. But she briefly considered other solutions where she could put her talent to full use. She suggested to other OSS division heads that she could be particularly useful by accompanying Allied troops who were heading off on missions to Central Europe and Czechoslovakia.

She also thought about heading back to the US so she could attend Officer Candidate School, which would solve the issue of rank once and for all. But that would mean leaving Rome and her work in MO, and she didn't want to bail on her team.

Then, in January 1945, after much wrangling and back-and-forth between MO staffers and military higher-ups, Zuzka was finally promoted to the rank of corporal.

* * *

With her promotion firmly in place, officers from other divisions within MO and OSS began to actively seek her out for their own projects. For instance, David C. Crockett, the finance and fiscal officer for the 2677th, sent Zuzka a memo asking for information on monetary intelligence in Czechoslovakia, as well as what kind of money the Russians were using in Budapest.

Being bumped up a rank was all well and good, but Zuzka still was stymied in many ways as her workload increased. "I wrote propaganda, recorded speeches, interrogated POWs, and bitched that my rank still did not correspond to my assignments and responsibilities," she said.

As before, her POW interrogations remained at the core of her duties, both for the military secrets she could pass along and the tidbits she could use to shape her own propaganda.

One afternoon shortly after her promotion, Zuzka was interrogating a surly POW who was a Nazi sergeant. After a few questions, he asked about her nationality. "Czech," she replied.

"Did you know that the Czechs and Slovaks are doing the Germans' dirty work along the Italian front?"

She perked up. "What do you mean?"

"Digging their ditches, washing their cars, and repairing their uniforms and shoes," he replied, explaining that there were thousands of Czech and Slovak soldiers who signed up to fight alongside the Nazis early in the war, but instead of going to battle, they were put to work at an abandoned farm near Livorno in northern Italy.

"How many are you talking about?" asked Zuzka. "Is it ten guys?"

"No, a couple hundred at least," he replied.

Well, this news was worth at least a couple of cigarettes. She lit one for herself and passed him another. As they puffed, Zuzka rolled the news of her fellow Czechs over in her mind. At least their lives were less at risk than if they were actively fighting, but she couldn't stand to see her countrymen oppressed and doing the Nazis' menial labor.

She finished her interrogations, and by the time she got back to Rome, she had her next project for Operation Sauerkraut all sketched out in her head: She would create speeches and a leaflet that would convince the Czechs and Slovaks at the Nazi work farm to surrender to the Allies.

The only Czech and Slovak typewriters in Italy were at the Vatican, so she camped out there for a couple of days to write five speeches and a ready-to-print leaflet in both languages in which she urged the conscripts to desert the Nazis and surrender to the Allies because the Germans were clearly losing the war. "Shed this German yoke of shame, cross over to the partisans," she implored them.

She recorded the speeches, which were broadcast throughout northern Italy with the help of the BBC's transmitters. Next, a small group of POWs were loaded up with the freshly printed leaflets and sent to Livorno to distribute the leaflets near the work farm.

All but a few of you used to be soldiers of the Czechoslovak army. Back then you were obedient to orders. So please be so again, here and now. The Czechoslovak army gives you only one command: Hit the Germans, wherever you are, whatever is in your powers. Do not hesitate, act now. Only one road leads to the homeland.

It took only a few days for a steady stream of Czechs and Slovaks to start to cross Allied lines to surrender and offer to fight against the Germans, and every single one of them pulled Zuzka's leaflet from their pockets or said they had heard one of her speeches on the radio. In all, more than six hundred Czech and Slovak soldiers deserted the German military as a result of her "yoke of shame" campaign.

* * *

While other OSS divisions could easily point to their successes—and failures—in terms of cities captured and enemy casualties, when it came to MO, the success of particular operations was harder to measure. The truth was it was exceedingly difficult to quantify the results of MO.

With the surrender of six hundred Czech soldiers, Zuzka had a great track record of MO wins, but the essence of MO could be compared to tossing a bottle with a note inside into the ocean: It was usually impossible to trace, and if you did hear back in the way of a POW divulging under interrogation that he'd seen a particular pamphlet, or Japanese soldiers surrendering while waving around a fake order from the emperor, those were the rare exceptions. Jane and Betty weren't as fortunate, and they often struggled with staying motivated and working long hours when it wasn't clear that their efforts were helping. In fact, the lack of visible results was so common within the propaganda arm that it even had a name: the MO Blues.

Zuzka's coworker Saul Steinberg was transferred to Washington in the fall of 1944, and in his new position, he was relieved to be free of the lack of feedback; DC headquarters had more officers overseeing their underlings. "Special Operations and Special Intelligence have something to show for their work, that is, you can see a bridge before and after it is blown up," he said. "With MO there is no way of measuring the effectiveness since the work which is accomplished is done without visible or measurable results, hence we can never tell how much MO influenced the enemy."

Bill Donovan still believed in the power of black propaganda, but the special commendation he sent to every MO worker in the 2677th regiment in the fall of 1944 was cold comfort for anyone caught in the throes of a severe case of the MO Blues.

According to Cora Du Bois, an anthropologist who was appointed acting chief of the Research & Analysis office in Ceylon— Sri Lanka today—the MO Blues were also endemic in other OSS divisions, including hers, though she clearly viewed the ability to run her own show to be worth it. "Almost everyone who one wanted to know was there," said Du Bois, the only woman to head up an OSS division. "But the actual assignments seemed pretty indefinite and what you did yourself, whether it had any influence or if anyone was paying any attention, one was never quite sure."

But for Betty, the essence of MO was what she had signed up for. "You don't get a body count when people change their minds or go over to the other side," she quipped.

*   *   *

As the year 1945 progressed, Zuzka continued writing propaganda, interrogating POWs, and providing colleagues with military intelligence, but it became clear that the war in Europe would soon be over. Allied firepower was easily defeating German troops, who were starting to retreat throughout the European theater.

She started to consider her next steps. Of course she was nervous and uncertain about the future: All four of the women were. They'd been entrusted with valuable work where they were able to call the shots for the first time in their lives. They were excited about the prospect of peace after some very dark years, but also nervous about their places in the postwar world.

One thing Zuzka knew for certain: She wouldn't be going back to her husband.

After months of silence from her husband, Charles, Zuzka arrived at work one day in April to find an envelope with her husband's familiar handwriting on her desk, pockmarked with censor stamps and postmarked from "somewhere in the South Pacific."

She opened the envelope with some ambivalence. After all, he'd never responded to an earlier letter she'd sent to tell him about her promotion to corporal after months of wrangling. She wasn't surprised, given the difficulty of military mail service, but in all honesty, she felt like she was just going through the motions, even though she had begun to doubt that they'd ever be reunited. The idea of returning to housewifely responsibilities paled next to the current thrill of her work and responsibilities.

Inside the envelope she found a brief cover letter along with a divorce decree.

Zuzka carefully folded the paper and tucked it back in the envelope. She wasn't shocked: All around her, men and women were sending and receiving Dear John and Jane letters to and from girlfriends and wives, boyfriends and husbands back home and stationed abroad. Living through the stress of wartime—and never knowing if you'd make it through to the other side—was one issue, but viewed through the filter of wartime trauma and chaos, it turned out that the previous relationships weren't that great after all, as Zuzka had discovered.

But lately something else was shifting. Previously, the divorces and affairs of her coworkers were largely the result of an uncertainty about the war's direction: After all, "Tomorrow we may be dead" was the line that higher-ups had regularly used on Zuzka in their efforts to have a little nighttime fun before heading off to battle the next morning. However, since the New Year, many affairs and new relationships had launched with a new burst of euphoria as it became clear that the enemy was losing. The devil-may-care attitude was still there, only now, in the spring of 1945, it assumed a more joyous air.

Instead of being upset by the letter, Zuzka was relieved. Her marriage was over, and her next decision would be hers and hers alone: Would she stay in the Army, or would she leave? Initially, she wanted to remain in the military, but only if she could receive the promotion in rank and pay that she so richly deserved. Just as her MO unit had packed up in Algiers a little more than a year earlier when the winds of war shifted, now many MO and OSS units were shifting their attention to the war in the Pacific, where it was clear that Japan was faltering.

But she wasn't crazy about the idea of heading to China. For one, she wasn't familiar with the culture or the language. She also wasn't thrilled with the prospect of returning to the States, another culture she was unfamiliar with, and where she'd still be another Damned Foreigner. "I wanted desperately to stay in Europe," she admitted.

She and her MO team decided to try once more for a promotion for her, and if that came through, it would cement her decision to stay in the military and perhaps finally go to Officer Candidate School to eliminate any future chaos concerning her rank.

And if it didn't, she expected she would be hired to work on the rebuilding efforts in Austria due to her fluency in the German language.

As before, her requests for promotion were heartily approved by her MO supervisors, exemplified in one memo:

> She has the best individual success record of any MO employee, her leaflets being accountable for some thousand enemy surrenders. Hard-working, intelligent, she suffered many frustrations in attempts to win a commission but weathered it and came up smiling. Loyal, untiring, efficient, she did valued liaison and other work not called for by her rank of corporal.

The personnel officer didn't agree and downgraded her evaluation by jotting a question mark next to the note about "her leaflets being accountable for 600 enemy surrenders."

This last bit particularly stung since she had just been awarded the Bronze Star on April 6, 1945, specifically due to her work on the Sauerkraut operation that resulted in the large numbers of Czechs and Slovaks surrendering to the Allies.

She and her colleagues were thoroughly disgusted by the refusal to recognize her tangible contributions, and finally, with the end of the war rapidly approaching, they gave up. In late April, she withdrew her application for promotion and instead filed papers for her discharge.

The world events that took over in the following week solidified both her decision and future path. On April 29, Germany agreed to withdraw its forces from Italy in the Surrender of Caserta. The next day, Hitler died by suicide. On May 7, 1945, Germany unconditionally surrendered to the Allies in Reims, France, formally ending World War II and the reign of the Third Reich.

Zuzka was determined to travel to Czechoslovakia to learn

how—*if*—her family had made it through the war. Brno, her hometown, had been liberated on April 24, but she hadn't received any news from them in several years, and by 1945, they had been living under German occupation for six years.

Then, to her great surprise, the Army promoted Zuzka once more. She assumed the title of sergeant right before her discharge on June 19. She'd take it.

The war was over, and so was her career in the US Army.

Chapter 10

Marlene

Not everyone agreed with Donovan's choice to use Marlene as a vocalist on the MUZAK Project. Many Germans—civilian and military alike—considered her a traitor to their country, and the Nazis had put a price on her head. But Donovan maintained that featuring her in the operation would be a masterful stroke, a perfect way to underscore just how much the Germans had lost under Hitler.

According to Betty, Marlene was the only one involved in the project who knew the true purpose of the recordings. "Donovan felt he could trust her and that she would appreciate what we were doing," she said years later. "I think Marlene made it better *because* she knew."

Despite the fact that everything was top secret, the first recording session was scheduled for August 16, 1944, at a studio in the middle of Times Square. It was mere blocks away from where Marlene rehearsed for her USO show. The musicians, studio techs, and other singers needed a special pass to get in, as did conductor Jimmy Carroll, who would go on to write the theme song to the *Mighty Mouse* cartoon series a decade later.

As orchestra members trickled in and began to tune their instruments, Marlene reviewed the lyric sheets for each of the four songs she would sing that day: "Mean to Me," "Time on My Hands," "Miss

Otis Regrets," and "Lili Marlene." Each song was labeled with several letters to show the nature of the song and how it would fit in with MO programming overseas. For instance, "Time on My Hands" had *B*, *S*, and *NOP* next to it on the master song list. *B* stood for Ballad, *S* was for Sentimental, while *NOP* meant No Propaganda Content.

There was another abbreviation that only appeared next to a handful of the three hundred songs that were recorded and distributed by MO: *SL*, short for Special Lyrics, which meant that the words in the song had been specifically altered to demoralize the listener. Lyricist—and OSS agent—Lothar Metzl was working overtime to translate American popular songs into German, and whenever a literal translation wasn't possible, he injected a slightly pessimistic meaning into the words. Occasionally, he took such liberties that his reworked lyrics barely resembled the original song.

The entire project violated US copyright laws and also went against the American Federation of Musicians, the union that represented the bulk of instrumentalists who played for recording sessions and live performances. OSS heads were concerned about copyright laws, but they couldn't request permission to reproduce and broadcast their work since the entire operation was kept confidential for security purposes.

Marlene ended up changing the words on almost every one of the songs she sang anyway, including "Taking a Chance on Love," which she recorded during her second OSS session on August 17. The song was classified as *B*, *S*, and *SS*, for Slightly Slanted.

First, the original lyrics:

> Here I go again
> I hear those trumpets blow again
> All aglow again
> Taking a chance on love.
>
> All things are mending now
> I see a rainbow blending now

We'll have a happy ending now
Taking a chance on love.

Marlene sang:

The moon looks into the valley
Where the birch trees grow
Don't ask me why, my love,
We will never meet again.

I don't know what will happen
All I know is that our song is ended.
And the moon will forever look into the valley
And far away, where the hills roll down to the sea
There will be a cross on a grave,
Red in the setting sun.

And then there was "Lili Marlene," which was classified as *B*, *NOP*, and *N*—for Nostalgic—along with *SL*.

This song had special meaning to her. "Lili Marlene" was based on "The Song of a Young Sentry," a poem written during World War I by a German soldier who was missing his sweetheart back home. By the late 1930s, it had been set to music and renamed "Lili Marlene," and somewhere along the way it became a chameleon of a song, its interpretation varying depending on your nationality, your stance on the war, and whether you were listening to the English or German version. To Germans, it served as a melancholy ballad, while as "Lily of the Lamplight" by the Brits, it morphed into a song about a prostitute.

The original first and fourth verses:

Outside the barracks, by the corner light
I'll always stand and wait for you at night
We will create a world for two

I'll wait for you the whole night through
For you, Lili Marlene
For you, Lili Marlene

When we are marching in the mud and cold
And when my pack seems more than I can hold
My love for you renews my might
I'm warm again, my pack is light
It's you, Lili Marlene
It's you, Lili Marlene

The orchestra was cued up, lips to mouthpieces, flecks of rosin dancing in the air. With one manicured hand Marlene caressed the silver microphone that could be easily mistaken for a grenade in the dark, while a Lucky Strike dangled from her other hand. It was wartime, but a girl still had to have her nails done, at least while she was in the States.

She lowered her head as if in prayer; she needed a moment to collect her thoughts. First, her family back in Germany. She knew that what she was about to do could be signing their death sentence.

That is, of course, if they were still alive.

But then, her boys. The reason she felt so utterly alive. She reached into her pocket and lightly tapped her standard-issue GI Zippo lighter made out of airplane metal.

"There's something about an American soldier you can't explain . . ."

Marlene glanced at Metzl's lyrics and came up with a few impromptu twists of her own, filtering the song through the eyes of a soldier in the final throes of an unwinnable war, who knows that he's going to lose not only his girl but his life as well.

She nodded at conductor Jimmy Carroll as he lifted his baton, launching the orchestra into the introduction. Marlene took a final drag on her cigarette and picked a fleck of tobacco off her tongue. She crushed out her Lucky, exhaled, and gave the lyrics her own

particular spin, her voice still husky due to the aftereffects of pneumonia.

> The lantern burns every night.
> It knows the steps . . . and the way you walk.
> It burns every night, but I've been long forgotten.
> Should harm come to me,
> Who will stand with you under the lantern?
> With you, Lili Marlene.
> With you, Lili Marlene.

When she finished, she closed her eyes to compose herself.

The air was charged with emotion and grief. The musicians sat
unmoving as the last notes faded away. They all wanted to savor this
moment, for the magic to linger. Most, if not all of them, didn't understand a word that she sang, but then again, they didn't have to.

German was her first language, but she hadn't had much chance
to use it since leaving Germany more than a decade earlier. Singing in her native language had brought everything back to her in
a rush.

She was singing for her *Mutter* and *Schwester* still in Germany;
she didn't know if she should be grieving them now.

For her two *Väter* and much-loved *Onkel*, all long dead.

For the rich life of her beloved 1920s Berlin.

It was all gone. Everything just existed in her mind now. She
needed a moment to bridge the years.

She opened her eyes, took a deep drag on her Lucky, and nodded
to Jimmy Carroll.

"Perfect," he said.

*   *   *

Marlene recorded twelve songs in all, over three sessions, all in
German. The tapes were pressed into acetate and shipped overseas
to MO headquarters in London. They were beamed into Germany

within weeks of Marlene's sessions. Marlene's daughter, Maria Riva, also sang at the MUZAK Project sessions.

The reaction from within Germany was immediate. "Officials felt that Marlene was a traitor, betraying her country by singing these songs that so upset many people listening," said Betty. "And yet we heard too that these songs seemed to be very popular, many said that they were overcome by this music and loved to hear her voice." Many even admitted that discovering that Marlene was singing for their enemy didn't diminish the pleasure of hearing her sing.

*   *   *

The day after the last sessions ended, Marlene flew directly to Paris, which was auspicious timing because on the following day, August 25, 1944, the city was liberated by the Allies.

Marlene was right there in the streets celebrating with everyone. The entire population was cheering and yelling, and Marlene was swept up in the jubilation. She visited the Hermès store, where she ended up spending hours signing autographs for the giddy crowd. When she had exhausted the store's limited stash of pencils, which had become a rare find during the war, she used her lipstick.

Kismet was released in theaters within days of the liberation of Paris, and though production had wrapped up only eight months before, the moviemaking business felt worlds away from her current life.

*   *   *

Donovan's instincts had been spot-on. With Marlene's songs broadcast nightly directly into Germany, her voice rubbed salt in the wounds of the Nazis, especially "Lili Marlene."

The Nazis fought back with a different rendition of "Lili Marlene," sung by German vocalist Lale Andersen. It was broadcast on Nazi radio stations every night at 9:57 P.M., forging brief and fragile cease-fires nightly as men in the trenches on both sides dropped their guns for a few minutes. But it was Marlene's interpretation that affected German morale to a greater degree. And so Soldatensender doubled down on broadcasting her version along with the other songs she'd recorded for MO, including "Miss Otis Regrets" and "Time on My Hands."

With her songs in heavy rotation throughout Germany, Marlene resumed touring with the USO in September 1944. She was ecstatic to be with her beloved GIs again and signed on for six months. Back on tour, Marlene was in her element. Unlike her first USO tour, this one was grittier and far more dangerous, especially since she had to embed herself with the troops on the front lines.

The tour launched at US bases in the north: Labrador, Greenland, and Iceland. She packed her winter uniform, but it didn't appear to help with the extreme cold, and it was only September.

The cold affected her immensely. The Army supplied her, like the rest of the troops, with long underwear, and thick pants and gloves. "The long underwear is the only thing that keeps my legs warm in this snow and mud," she said.

They traveled in open-air jeeps since the Germans tended to attack closed jeeps more often than open ones. "We drove pretty fast and I never wore gloves and our shoes were wet and it was always cold and rainy," she said. "It wasn't easy, but it was wonderful."

But when it came time for her shows, even if it was blowing snow, she always ditched the long underwear and heavy overcoat and changed into a thin sequined gown. After all, she felt that she couldn't perform all wrapped up in a heavy overcoat; since her boys were making extreme sacrifices, so could she.

In the bombed-out ruins where she hunkered down with her fellow soldiers, Marlene scarfed down cold C rations, careful to keep one hand free to swat away the skeletal rats that weren't shy about asking for food. At base camp, the fare was mostly hot dogs and sauerkraut. And they always ate outside; that way, they could see the bombs coming. "Even when there was an indoors, we ate outdoors, with rain on the food and cold grease running down," she said.

Sleep, when she could manage it, was either in a cold barracks, a damp sleeping bag in a frozen field, or sprawled across the back seat of a jeep. And she washed her face in a helmet with melted snow just like the other soldiers.

"She's worked herself to death trying to entertain the troops," said Richard Gully, a soldier who served as her escort for part of the tour.

Most of the other stars on the USO tours took the safe route, minding their handlers, never straying from the stage, and interacting with soldiers only from the stage, then retreating into armored vehicles while the band members were still putting their instruments away.

Marlene was different. Not only could she not get enough time with her boys, but she wanted to bear witness to the sheer destruction of the war and visit with the soldiers who were fighting at the front and had it the worst. The troops deeply respected her as a result.

"She pushed the limits," said Colonel Barney Oldfield, a war correspondent and press officer, who worked with Marlene during the second USO tour. "If she wanted to go towards the front lines the driver looked the other way," he remembered, adding that some of the troops she greeted thought they were seeing a mirage when they caught sight of her in their hellhole of a war zone. "Here is this glamorous figure from Hollywood coming towards you, and you pinch yourself to realize you're not having hallucinations."

Some soldiers must have gotten downright delusional when Marlene decided to hold a free-for-all kissing event at some of the shows. At one show in Paris, a journalist reported that "her forehead got so bruised by the helmets of the eager GIs that she had to issue a 'hats off' request."

* * *

At the beginning of 1945, the war was at a critical juncture. Over the winter, increasing numbers of German soldiers were surrendering to the Allies. To replenish their ranks, the Nazis began to draft teenage boys and elderly men into the war.

The Germans were losing, they *knew* they were losing, and as a result they were desperate. They lashed out, baring their teeth and indiscriminately attacking whoever got in the way . . . especially German movie stars who had switched their allegiance to the enemy.

Marlene became even more of a prize target for Hitler, who would regard her capture as a military coup and a disaster for the Allies. The Nazis were keeping close tabs on her travels on the USO tour, which often skirted dangerously close to the front lines. Indeed, during the Battle of the Bulge, as the Third Army moved into Germany, Marlene barely escaped with her life when a German counterattack struck only a kilometer away from her camp.

She waved away her officers' concerns at the dangers. She admitted, though, that while she had no fear of death, she was afraid of being captured and held prisoner. If the Nazis captured her, she knew she'd be mercilessly tortured with the results paraded for all to witness. "They'll shave off my hair, stone me, and have horses drag me through the streets, or worse, force me to talk on the radio."

General George Patton had presented her with a pearl-handled revolver identical to his. "It's small, but it's effective," he told her, leaving no doubt that he meant for her to use it on herself, if the circumstances required.

The shows were different this time around as well. Traveling—and performing—was far more dangerous for everyone involved, so everything had to be even more structured, with more precautions taken in advance. The dangerous, cold, and brutal living conditions endeared her to the soldiers even more.

"It'll do the soldiers good to know that you're at the front," General Patton had told her before she embarked on her second USO tour. "They'll tell themselves the situation can't be so bad if Marlene Dietrich's there. If we were all going to be mowed down here, the old man certainly wouldn't expose her to such danger."

The joy she brought whenever she showed up was palpable, making the hardships she faced worth it. "When the boys think we won't come because the shelling is heavy, and then we arrive, that's the greatest thrill," she said.

To her boys, she was mother, sister, and lover, all wrapped up in one. From childhood, Marlene loved to show affection to family and friends by cooking for them; they particularly clamored for her scrambled eggs. But here, at yet another undisclosed location in war-torn Western Europe, kitchens were in short supply, let alone eggs. So she displayed her affection in other ways. Inevitably, at one point in her USO routine, she'd mention that people were always asking her if she had ever slept with Eisenhower. She'd pause and slowly scan the crowd with her famous bedroom eyes before unleashing the punch line:

"Darling, Ike wasn't at the front."

The GIs absolutely adored her, fighting over the chance to commandeer a spare jeep for a three A.M. joyride or to share her sleeping bag.

Or to hold her head while she puked. Marlene was particularly sensitive to exhaust fumes from the Army trucks, and she spent her time overseas in a constant state of nausea. Sometimes a slug or two of Calvados helped—more often than not, it came right back up—but she refused to abandon her boys.

The venues became more precarious as well, whether she was performing in a bombed-out movie theater, waiting on a food line, or riding in the back of an open-air truck while inhaling diesel fumes.

Plus, she never knew where she'd be from one day to the next, jumping around from Belgium to France, then to Italy as Allies continued their push forward. All the while, the number of German troops surrendering increased, and she soon added another job to her roster: interpreter.

Several US officers asked her if she could talk with a few POWs who were officers, if they could tell her anything that could benefit Allied troops at that point in the war. While it must have been surreal for the German officers to be interrogated by Marlene, the tactic worked, and she was able to pass along some critical bits of information to the Allies.

Once they made it into Germany, Marlene was shocked to see

the devastation and destroyed villages and towns, but she had no pity for those who were responsible for the damage. "I hate to see all these ruins, but I believe Germany deserves everything that's happening now," she admitted.

Apparently not every German hated her for going over to the other side. One day Marlene was preparing to perform in a theater in a small German town, and the theater owner bustled around to make her feel as comfortable as possible. "The owner of the theater was in a frenzy of excitement at the famous Dietrich playing in his house," said soldier Richard Gully.

In fact, when she arrived in Germany, she decided she was done with acting; her life during wartime had shown her what was really important. "I am through with Hollywood," she said. "After entertaining troops for a full year, I know I couldn't go back to motion pictures."

Maria Riva attested to this. "She was a very, very intelligent woman," she said. "One of the reasons she hated being a movie star was because being a movie star didn't need intelligence, as far as she was concerned. She rather looked down her nose at all movie stars anyway."

And then, suddenly, it was over. Unlike the euphoria she had felt when she announced D-Day to thousands of cheering soldiers, Marlene had mixed emotions when she heard of Hitler's suicide on April 30, 1945, followed by Germany's surrender a week later.

Of course she was absolutely thrilled to know that Hitler was finally gone, but like the other women, she feared the end of the war meant she would no longer be useful.

She offered to go to the Pacific theater, where USO tours were still active, but the Army ordered her to get some rest first.

* * *

Marlene may have felt like she no longer had a purpose, but according to Betty, that was far from true. "Lili Marlene" was still resonating and affecting soldiers who were trying to win the war against Japan. Plus, it wasn't just the troops who loved the song.

When Betty was transferred behind enemy lines to Kunming, China, in early 1945, she and the other MO staffers had to adjust to an extremely isolated existence. Back in Washington, Jane wanted to help boost the spirits of her far-flung colleagues, and so when some extra records from Marlene's secret MO sessions in Times Square showed up at OSS headquarters in Washington, Jane decided to send a few to her friend Betty in China. Maybe they'd cheer her up along with the others.

"These great big records arrived, and we played them on a very squeaky record player," Betty recalled. "Sometimes we'd even dance to some of the music, it was so wonderful to be able to relax. But whenever 'Lili Marlene' came on, we'd always stop dancing and just listen. It was so poignant and beautifully sung, it was just soul-wrenching to everyone. It made everyone kind of homesick and war-weary, not just the Germans."

Chapter 11

Jane

With her promotion firmly in hand, Jane added yet another task to her plate as she signed on to Project Marigold, a supersecret operation based in midtown Manhattan, a few blocks from where Marlene practiced her USO act. The unit employed twelve *issei*, or first-generation Japanese-American writers, editors, typesetters, and artists who were required to write, design, and print several finished leaflets each week, ready to distribute throughout the China-Burma-India theater.

As was the case for Zuzka in Italy, leaflets were the ideal form of propaganda for a variety of reasons. In early 1944, the OSS recognized that leaflets were the best form of black propaganda to use with German troops in Italy, who were short on food, ammo, and reading material, and eagerly devoured any bit of written material they could get their hands on. In fact, many held on to them as a kind of souvenir and read them repeatedly. By 1945, Japanese troops were in a similar position, and now that it appeared that the tide had turned against the Japanese, any MO campaigns going forward were going to rely heavily upon these simple sheets of paper with powerful words.

The black propaganda was aimed at soldiers as well as civilians in those parts of China that were occupied by Japanese troops. In the 1940s, China's literacy rate hovered around 20 percent, so the majority of propaganda had to be in the form of drawings and graphics. And since Japan had long directed its own black propaganda toward the Chinese, OSS leaflets had to be equally compelling.

While the words and text were simple, the planning and design was anything but.

"A good layout is as important as a good text," an MO directive instructed. "No good leaflet can be composed simply by writing down what you want to say and then asking a printer to print it. A good leaflet has a double impact: the initial impact on the casual passerby, which must convey its main message at first glance; and the delayed impact on the careful reader, which must provide him with food for thought when he has time to read it through in latrines. Pictures, captions and display are at least 50 percent of the value of any leaflet. The writer who disregards this is a menace to leafleteering."

Marigold's efforts were designed to supplement those of Betty's group, which was hampered by a small team and inadequate supplies and printing facilities. It was expensive to ship large quantities of leaflets via military pouch, but it was thought to be more reliable and consistent. When Betty received the shipments, she'd pass them on to other OSS teams to distribute throughout the theater. The New York–based team also occasionally prepared scripts for black radio broadcasts into Japan.

There were many challenges to get the operation up and running. First, staffing the New York office. Marigold required native Japanese and Chinese speakers who also had some experience working in the news media, either newspapers or magazines or radio, and who had lived in the United States. Of course the US government had forcibly removed over 110,000 Japanese-Americans—both Japanese- and American-born—from their homes and relocated them to ten internment camps, mostly in the West. In order to staff up for Project Marigold, OSS officials canvassed the camps for people with suitable experience. Several staffers were recruited from Heart Mountain, a camp in Wyoming, while others had worked at Japanese newspapers and radio stations in New York and California.

Just as Zuzka took a risk in walking through a tent flap to interrogate German POWs, Jane and other OSS staffers working on Project Marigold had to know they could trust their Japanese coworkers. There was always a chance, though slim, that they could be spying for Japan or intent on sabotaging the Americans' projects in response to their forced internment, so all prospective Marigold employees were thoroughly screened over the course of several weeks.

"To get the Japanese personnel to cooperate we had to bend to their ideas, not the other way around," Colonel Herbert Little wrote in a report about the project. "The Japanese were not interested in an overwhelming victory over Japan, but in ending the war and building for a democratic future. They distinguished between the Japanese military clique and the Japanese people themselves, and so our propaganda therefore emphasized the inevitability of defeat, the advantages of cessation of hostilities, and hopes for a democratic and peace-loving Japan in the future."

The question of where to locate the unit quickly became an issue. The idea of having a group of Japanese men working at OSS headquarters in Washington was unacceptable. Besides, housing continued to be a problem in the capital through the end of the war. What about New York? There were already small pockets of Japanese neighborhoods throughout the boroughs, so a small group of Japanese men was less likely to attract undue attention—or violence—there than in Washington. Besides, some of the candidates already lived in the city.

While Jane was still mad at the Japanese who had held her and her family hostage for more than six months, she had the utmost respect for the Japanese-American citizens she worked alongside at the OSS. After all, they were both on the same team.

*　*　*

In addition to her other job responsibilities, Jane often traveled to New York City to oversee production of the Marigold leaflets that were bound for the Far East. She also created a number of leaflets on her own; as was the case with her Rumor Mill sessions, she clearly relished coming up with ideas for the project. What follows are two orders that she wrote and produced.

```
TARGET: Japanese Troops
SUBJECT: Factory Accidents
PURPOSE: Alarm troops regarding women's working
conditions
MEDIUM: Leaflet
PURPORTED SOURCE: Women's Dept. Committee for
Re-establishment of Labor Unions
TIMING: Any Time
QUANTITY & DISTRIBUTION: Sent to field/3000
DATE: August 23, 1944
TRANSLATION: Accidents have increased because of
long hours, late night work, insufficient training and
compulsory increased production.
```

The artwork shows a woman working at a piece of machinery, an up-and-down saw, with blood dripping from her arm. The translation is superimposed in the upper left-hand corner of the picture.

```
TARGET: Japanese Women
SUBJECT: Neglected Children
PURPOSE: Worry women (and troops) regarding homefront
conditions
MEDIUM: Leaflet
PURPORTED SOURCE: Women War Workers
TIMING: Any Time
QUANTITY & DISTRIBUTION: Sent to field/3000
DATE: August 23, 1944
TRANSLATION: Mothers work at the factories while
children remain at home. Accidents may happen to
the children. Who will take care of the children of
working mothers?
```

The illustration shows a teenage boy holding an empty rice bowl and a window behind him shows smokestacks off in the distance, while children sleep nearby.

But perhaps Jane's greatest accomplishment in Morale Operations was refining a black propaganda version of the Japanese field service code manual, or *Senjin Kun*, which was based on the original hardcover version that had been distributed to every member of the Japanese military since January 1941. *Senjin Kun* provided Japanese soldiers with rules about conduct and behavior on and off the battlefield.

```
TOPIC: SENJIN KUN [Battlefield Code]
MEDIUM: Visual—26 page booklet
TARGET: Mainly Japanese armed forces, limited quantity
for civilians
PURPORTED SOURCE: Study Group to carry out Battlefield
Code
INTELLIGENCE DATA SOURCE: Captured "Military Manual
for stand-by and Secondary Reserves" which contains
the original "Senjin Kun" text. Also, captured
"Soldier's Pocket Ledger" for imitation of cover and
design material.
REMARKS: This project was originated in China and
brought back by Lt. Col. Little. He designated the
cover design and type of material to be used. The
format, cover as well as the size of types are exact
reproductions of the original to give an authentic
appearance. The text of the introduction printed on
pages 1—2 of the booklet is authentic. However, from
page 3 on, it is a parody of the original text and
is full of satire phrases with double meanings . . .
which are cleverly expressed and comprehensible to all
Japanese soldiers. In our English translation we have
tried to integrate the feeling and spirit of the code
rather than the exact phraseology.
```

Senjin Kun had been published in the wake of the Nanking Massacre, when Japanese troops captured the Chinese city in 1937 and proceeded to rape and murder an estimated two hundred thousand civilians over the course of six weeks. The rampage shocked the world, and the Japanese military, perhaps to appease the opinion that had turned against them, published the manual and distributed it to every soldier in order to prevent a similar atrocity in the future.

Repeated throughout the original pocket-sized manual was the message that to surrender to the enemy was a despicable act that would bring great shame upon a soldier's family as well as the emperor. Betty and her team had already created black propaganda undermining that message, and Jane decided to follow suit with an enormously ambitious project: to reproduce copies of *Senjin Kun* as a work of satire, with subtle twists throughout, telling the soldier that it was, in fact, a very honorable act to surrender to the enemy.

A committee of MO members loved the idea and signed off on it, but they had their doubts, both about the project itself and who could possibly pull it off. Fortunately, the manual didn't have to resemble a carbon copy of the original. As the war progressed and supplies grew scarce within Japan, the military resorted to using cheaper, coarser paper for reprints, and the quality of the cover was rougher as well. But the most important part was the text itself. Like other forms of propaganda, it couldn't appear that the enemy had produced it.

Here's one example from the satiric *Senjin Kun*: "Number Three: Military Discipline. The entire force should move as one in response to a command, an essential requisite of a single general's winning fame, even though 100 thousand men perish . . . Especially on the battlefield, complete obedience is necessary. When a command is given in the face of great danger, one must immediately and cheerfully fling himself into the jaws of death without thought, even though he may die like a dog or face public ridicule later."

Or this: "Number Six: Aggressiveness. We should be constantly aggressive in combat. Act boldly, disregarding everything: Consider your body as light as a hair in the rectum even though your corpse may rot in the field, for according to the instruction of an ancient, our guide is: 'I wish to die where the Emperor farts.'"

And finally: "Simplicity and Fortitude: Life on the battlefield must be plain. As to your food, be satisfied with pickled plums and sloppy rice. Never envy the food supplies of armed forces of foreign countries. Luxury is not for Japanese soldiers, it is for the upper class at home who toast in luxurious tea houses the valor of the Japanese soldier in the field."

A total of three hundred copies of this false *Senjin Kun* were printed. Jane sent a few copies to Betty in Delhi, and they tossed a few ideas back and forth about additional distribution. Even though they were located on the opposite side of the globe from each other, Jane and Betty corresponded regularly and worked together on projects, depending upon the expeditiousness of the pouches coming and going between Washington and India.

"We can use a steady flow of war photographs, anything dealing with Japanese defeat, materiel, prisoners of war, and personalities," Betty wrote in one memo. "I had in mind the tear-jerker pictures shown recently of US soldiers with Japanese kids on Saipan. Maybe somebody could contact OSS picture sources. Have the 8X10 glossies copied and send us the negatives. We have developing facilities here, although we would make R&A happy if we could contribute some reams of Eastman Velor Bromide paper, size 8X10."

Senjin Kun was smuggled into northern Burma behind Japanese lines, and given the feedback received, the guide succeeded. "It's believed to be one of the more useful [pieces of propaganda] yet produced to subvert the morale of Japanese troops," Herbert S. Little wrote in a memo.

* * *

Despite the crushing workload, Jane loved working on Marigold. She was wildly creative, and the sky was the limit when it came to coming up with ideas so far-fetched that they might just work. Best of all, no one was censoring her.

She also helped to brainstorm ideas for composite photos for Marigold distribution. A memo describes one photo as a garden party attended by Tojo and Admiral Shimada. "This is being made into a [triptych]; on one side [of the garden party] will be a scene in a mine where women are working. On the other side, dead soldiers.

"The next is a beauty: on one side is a golfing scene with Prince Tokugawa, Tojo, and Shimada next to a picture showing workers chained to machines." Since photo-editing software wasn't around back then, once the ideas were approved, an artist in the New York Marigold office gathered up the art and photos before painstakingly cutting and pasting the art into a montage by hand.

Jane also planned a number of cartoons to be drawn by Marigold artists. One portrayed Japanese prime minister and general Hideki Tojo in the form of an octopus, all eight arms stretched across a map of the Far East, with a few arms being hacked off.

Another cartoon—"What is our Imperial Navy Doing?"—pitted two different branches of the military against each other, picturing an army officer nervously poring over a map that shows the enemy getting closer. The caption accuses the navy of incompetence in defending the island nation.

Jane also came up with the idea for the booklet "Physical Training Guide for Industrial Workers," allegedly published by Dai Nippon Athletic Association. The guide was a small booklet that encouraged wartime factory employees to take regular exercise breaks during their workday, with the express purpose of slowing production on assembly lines.

In addition to producing leaflets, Jane and the team also planned and designed fake newspapers and magazines aimed at different demographic groups. Each magazine had to include advertisements, editorial masthead, and contact information for the publisher, which had to be an actual business address. *Flowers of Japan* was a twenty-four-page magazine about Japanese art, while *New Japan* was a newsmagazine supposedly published by an underground group of war resisters with plans to overthrow the imperial government. The unit even planned *Friend*, a magazine for children featuring cartoons, poems, and letters from children sent to their soldier fathers.

Many of the projects for Marigold never reached their intended targets, or even went into production, which was most often due to a shortage of personnel and office space in both New York and Washington. But a highly inefficient work process also played a role.

Once a leaflet or cartoon was approved, the Washington MO desk would often send a sample to Betty so she and others could sign off on it. Despite her unit being moved to Calcutta in order to be closer to the field, it didn't necessarily mean that supplies and samples reached them any faster. Sometimes the shipment was stuck on a loading dock in Washington or on a landing strip somewhere along the way, left outside during monsoon season, or waylaid on the return trip.

And even though there was a printing press in Calcutta, it was broken more often than it was operational, and replacement parts were usually delayed. Plus, the electric grid was spotty, running for only a few hours at a time, and the weather was so stiflingly hot that the ink and other chemicals used for printing boiled after being off-loaded from the ships, which made running the only press they had impossible.

Many times, given the restrictions on printing presses in close proximity to MO offices, Betty and the others would essentially prepare a camera-ready proof to send to Washington. The office there would print up the document and send copies back to the MO outpost. Of course this took an inordinate amount of time, but it was the only option for many projects at far-flung bases where supplies and equipment were in short supply. And when something in Washington went awry, it made everything all the worse, given the significant amount of time and resources expended.

Jane Foster, an MO agent based in Calcutta who frequently worked with Betty, spilled out her frustrations about the inefficiencies to a field agent in March of 1945. "Enclosed are the usual batch of Washington productions," she wrote. "Please note most of them are dated December 20. No wonder they are screaming when we fail to mention any of their ingenious ideas enclosed in letters which we never receive."

In another memo: "Jane [Smith-Hutton] will try to locate authentic paper in New York next weekend through staff at Marigold. She will also check with Shrewsbury to see what happened to her order for the production of Japanese paper requested *about eight months ago*."

In any case, a leaflet or cartoon could possibly hasten the end of the war, but logistics was clearly hampering efforts. While some solutions were floated—for instance, sending printed copies to the field without first receiving approval—some of the hindrances were of a political bent, and nothing that Jane or any of the other women could do would help.

Perhaps unnamed higher-ups were still sore that they didn't have final say on Marigold projects, no matter how much they were told that hewing to their own ideas could sabotage MO's efforts. It's possible that one or more of the officers with direct oversight of the Washington MO bureau—and who had turned down Jane's applications for promotion—started to retaliate, unhappy with the willy-nilly, haphazard ways in which Morale Operations thrived. There was also a chance that Donovan instructed some of the men in charge to press for concrete results, to ensure that his beloved OSS would continue after victory in the Asian theater when the time came to plead for additional resources in the postwar era.

In any event, micromanagement started to become the rule at the MO Washington office. In the spring of 1945, Jane was ordered to keep a weekly log tracking every single letter and report that was sent to the office from agents in the field, as well as those who she forwarded the letters to. With hundreds, maybe thousands of letters and reports coming in each week, it's difficult not to view this as petty retaliation. Another memo went out ordering her and the other desk heads to send any secretary or typist with a spare hour to an officer's office, which, of course, since they were understaffed to begin with, was an impossible scenario.

Jane loved her job, but like Zuzka, she was becoming increasingly disillusioned by the politics that clearly favored the contributions of men. Even as it was clear that the war would soon be over—and she'd be out of a job—she continued to fight for more money and a job title that more accurately described what her work responsibilities actually entailed, perhaps as a form of her own retaliation.

In June of 1945, she applied for a promotion from her current CAF-9 level to CAF-12, which would give her the title of operations officer with a commensurate salary of $4500. "This classification puts me on same pay level as [Michael E.] Choukas," she penciled in the margins of the cover letter accompanying her application, referring to a coworker who she felt did the same tasks and who joined the OSS almost a year after she did, starting as operations officer level CAF-11 with a salary of $3800. "Hope these #s are what the Coliseum wants. Yes! Yes!" she added.

But her request was turned down just two days later. "It should be pointed out that under the present promotional policy Jane would not be eligible for a promotion until at least January 1, 1946," the response said, though Jane had witnessed exceptions being made for male employees.

She was becoming increasingly fed up, but also torn as to whether she should resign early or wait until the end of the war. And then an edict came down from on high that Jane's beloved weekly Rumor Mill sessions would be discontinued.

"The Rumor Committee is dissolved," the memo from Major Andre Pacatte began. "Based on Weekly MO directives, each desk head will work on rumors purely on the creative basis while reading daily intelligence material. As these rumors are created, a list should be sent to the Panel for discussion."

For Jane, that was the last straw. She carried on for a couple of months more, but the writing was on the wall. In early July, Colonel Little sent out an office memo discussing postwar plans for MO and the OSS. Perhaps he was one of the few who were in on US plans to bomb Hiroshima and Nagasaki, but the overall message he sent forth was that MO would be winding down, and he wrote about starting to integrate efforts between MO and the Office of War Information, which had issued white propaganda over the course of the war. "For security reasons, this should be [regarded] only in general and not as a plan," he wrote.

On August 1, 1945, Jane applied for a leave without pay, supposedly due to her health, though there are no indications that she was sick. Then, on August 17—eight days after the second atomic bomb was dropped on Nagasaki—she rescinded her leave and officially resigned from the OSS. Her tenure had lasted just eighteen months.

The war was over. She had no idea what would happen next.

Chapter 12

Betty

Betty landed in Calcutta in early January of 1945 and dove right into new projects, including one that Bill Magistretti had developed involving railway passes, supposedly from the official Japanese bureau of transportation. The passes, which contained messages instructing people living in cities to immediately escape to a rural area due to an immediate but unspecified threat, would ideally create panic among urban residents and cause them to flee the city.

Bill and Betty wrote and designed the passes, running them by several POWs to attest to the accuracy of the language and design. Once approved, they sent a final copy to Washington, which printed fifty pounds of passes and fifty pounds of messages to be stapled to the passes. They were then shipped to Calcutta to be air-dropped during a military maneuver.

They were just about to give them to agents to distribute into the field when Winifred Jub, a local resident working at the office, held one of the messages up to the light.

"Look at the pretty bird!" she said.

The others discovered that the "pretty bird" was, in fact, a watermark of an American eagle on the paper that was printed back in Washington. At least the mistake had been discovered before they were distributed, but Bill and Betty were livid: All of their hard work had to be scrapped.

"A considerable number of the white sheets to be attached to the passes bear the watermark of the seal of the United States, clearly identifying the origin," Bill wrote in a memo to the chief of the reproduction branch in DC. "Request that as of this date, all production for MO be prepared and printed on paper stock."

There was a reason why the China-Burma-India theater—or CBI—was often referred to as Confused Beyond Imagination.

*   *   *

Barely a month after Betty arrived in Calcutta, she received orders to transfer to the Allied base in Kunming in Yunnan Province, China, which was where she wanted to be in the first place.

On the surface, it made sense. Since the Japanese navy had ceased to be a real threat, attention had shifted to China, where a quarter of the land mass was presently occupied by the Japanese army. This was the pattern as the focus of OSS efforts in the CBI theater shifted in order to be closer to the action, in this case from Ceylon to China. Plus, Donovan rescinded the so-called order against sending OSS women into China.

As before, however, Betty knew not to hold her breath, knowing that military edicts and protocol—as well as rapidly changing events in the war in the Pacific theater—could alter plans in an instant. But one day in March of 1945, Betty stepped onto a C-47 military plane with thirty other passengers, bound for Kunming.

Military airplanes in the 1940s were not pressurized or heated. The only safety features were oxygen masks and parachutes. No food and drink, even water, was allowed on board.

Someone had scrawled IS THIS TRIP NECESSARY? across the nose of the plane, underscoring the danger of the voyage Betty was about to take across "the Hump," the main route across the Himalayas from Calcutta to Kunming. The Hump was known for violent storms, wind shears, and unpredictable squalls caused by crosswinds that could cause a plane to drop six thousand feet in altitude in less than ten seconds. It's estimated that between 1942 and 1945 more than three thousand American, British, and Chinese planes crashed while traveling over the Hump.

Two months before Betty's flight, a New Year's Eve storm had claimed twenty-six planes within a ten-hour span, so she prepared for the worst. "It was a terrible ride, about three hours of storms and lightning and jagged cliffs all around us," Betty later said. "You could look way down below and see all the little crosses scattered across the snow." The "crosses" were planes that hadn't made it.

Sitting across from her on the flight was an annoyingly calm woman named Julia McWilliams, who serenely read a book for the entire flight while most people closed their eyes, prayed, and/or got sick. McWilliams worked in the Research & Analysis branch of MO and would later be known as Julia Child, who introduced French cooking to Americans.

"I looked at my parachute and wondered what cord I should pull," Betty said, but she wasn't overly worried because she had a secret lucky charm in tow.

Back in Washington, a friend had given Betty a stuffed animal "gremlin" named Chester, and told her that if she came across a rough patch while traveling that she would survive as long as she had Chester. She clutched him tightly as soon as she stepped onto a plane, and though there were some scary moments, the plane always landed in one piece.

Since she had first headed overseas, she had told a few pilots about Chester. Back in Calcutta, she was at a dance when someone turned down the music and a man approached the microphone. "Is the owner of Chester here?" he asked.

Betty introduced herself and told him yes, Chester was hers. He told her he was a pilot and had to fly the Hump the next day. The weather forecast was grim, and he asked if Chester could accompany him on the flight.

"Of course!" she said. Chester made it there and back safely, and Betty would hold on to Chester for the rest of her life.

On her first flight over the Hump, they landed safely, though Betty was a bit shaken up by the nonstop turbulence. Before anyone was allowed off the plane, two airport employees walked on and sprayed the interior of the plane—and the passengers—with clouds of DDT, which was protocol for all military planes landing in China.

Betty and the others disembarked, choking and coughing from the pesticide, and walked right into the absolute culture shock that was China.

Roads in Kunming were lined on both sides with tall eucalyptus trees, but the pleasant astringent smell couldn't disguise the overwhelming stench that permeated the city, caused by the canals running alongside major roads that served as open sewers. Though residents used them as a water source, the canals were also often the final resting place for corpses, both human and animal.

Even more disconcerting was the fact that for the first time since she'd left the States, Betty was essentially behind enemy lines. Japan occupied great swaths of land in southeast China, and though the Japanese army had begun to retreat when Betty landed there in the spring of 1945, Kunming was in the crosshairs as a major Allied base.

"For the first time since Pearl Harbor in Hawaii I felt that a war was being fought not too many mountain bends away from me," she said. She and her colleagues were regularly briefed on the comprehensive evacuation plans designed to get them out if the Japanese decided to attack in the wake of retreat, or as a last-ditch kamikaze revenge mission.

At least in Kunming, Betty didn't have to worry about broken or nonexistent printing presses. Her job had shifted from writing printed leaflets and other documents to coming up with ideas for stories for the OSS radio station that was broadcasting into China. Betty's new Chinese colleagues were largely responsible for execution, production, and distribution; Betty and her American coworkers just had to brainstorm the ideas and target the people they wanted to influence, primarily the Chinese civilian population.

With the Japanese military starting to crumble and rebel, this was the moment that black propaganda was designed for: depress the morale of soldiers in the field and make it feel like further fighting would be futile, and demoralize Chinese civilians so they would stop supporting the war and perhaps even engage in a bit of sabotage toward their occupiers.

Betty hit the ground running, coming up with ideas for stories aimed at the Chinese population that were designed to increase their animosity toward the Japanese, though it was common knowledge that the Japanese would also be listening in. Since Betty's knowledge of the Chinese language was rudimentary, she cooked up ideas and rumors and handed them off to her Chinese coworkers in Kunming to translate and execute them.

For example, in the spring of 1945, Japanese kamikaze missions were ramping up as the Allies started to close in, and Betty discovered that the Japanese military was pressuring its Chinese soldiers to sign up for the suicide missions.

She asked a Chinese colleague what he thought. "We think they're crazy!" he replied. "Why die before your time?" Hmmmm, Betty thought, and she soon cooked up the Kamikaze Campaign, coming up with headlines like "Japanese Organize Chinese Suicide Squads to Fight Foreign Devils" for the MO-produced guerrilla Chinese newspaper and recruiting posters and leaflets from the nonexistent Kamikaze Induction Center that read, "You, Too Can Become a Human Limpet!" In the next few weeks, word traveled back about more than three hundred Chinese soldiers who had been working with the Japanese who surrendered to the Allies.

News of the success of Zuzka's League of Lonely War Women project eventually traveled to other MO outposts around the world, and Betty was inspired to produce a new batch of propaganda using the same theme. She drafted radio scripts and newspaper articles to announce a new program—supposedly instituted by the Japanese government—instructing single and married female civilians back home in Japan to become pregnant by any means possible so as to increase the population in the emperor's honor. And just like Zuzka's League of Lonely War Women missive, these "news" items were earmarked for distribution to Japanese soldiers, not civilian women.

Another served as a variation on the theme with a pamphlet that spelled out the horrors of what she referred to as "bomb loneliness," or the psychological trauma that Japanese women experienced back home as the result of aerial bombardments and attacks. The pamphlet was supposedly written by a well-known Tokyo physician and came with an official stamp of approval from the medical department of the Japanese army.

"The girl you left behind may never bear children again because of the shock to her nervous system," Betty wrote. "And she may also suffer from bombing neuroses which often expresses itself in maniacal desires to murder those dearest to her."

Though OSS outposts, including Kunming, were under constant guard, there was always a chance that a local agent was a counterspy and would suddenly turn on the Americans, or that errant gunfire between rival gangs would pierce the walls of their supposedly protected compound. In addition, some members of the local police force were not too thrilled with having Americans in their midst, and they occasionally took target practice by shooting at OSS staffers as they made their way around the city. Joy Homer, an MO colleague who had roomed with Betty back in Delhi, had been attending social events and interviewing diplomats at the Chinese embassy in Kunming looking for some dirt she could use. One night she was struck by an errant taxi driver who was linked to a Chinese diplomat and she suffered severe injuries. Such "accidents" involving Chinese drivers and OSS workers had become distressingly common toward the end of the war. Homer returned home to the United States to recover, but she died from her injuries a year later.

As a result, OSS higher-ups made a special effort to make life as easy as possible for Betty and the others, which included ramping up the entertainment options available. Unlike at her previous overseas posts, Betty and her coworkers actually got weekends off in Kunming, and she took every opportunity to travel to the nearby countryside, where she could soak in the hot springs and walk in the mountains even though poisonous snakes lurked and local residents observed a "shoot first" attitude when it came to strangers on their property.

Bloated corpses in canals aside, there were a number of good restaurants in Kunming as well as social gatherings and official functions organized by the military that MO staffers attended almost every night to blow off steam. Betty described the scene as "a sort of Cinderella nightlife that the American army strictly regulated with an 11 o'clock curfew."

Charles Fenn, an OSS colleague who would later write *At the Dragon's Gate*, a book about his experiences, remembered these parties, where each night approximately eighty men and thirteen women easily finished off three cases of rum and whiskey. "Betty was queen of the ball, and wore a dress so tight you could read her pulse," he wrote.

The parties served as a welcome, albeit temporary, antidote to the stress of work and life in a war zone. "Everything was uncertain and it was like being in limbo," Betty said. "And we were all very lonely."

Betty had lived apart from her husband, Alex, for over three years, and though he had also joined the OSS, the rule against married spouses serving in the same theater applied to them, so there was little chance that their paths would cross. "There was a lonesome side to everyone's life, stationed so far from home in an alien country," Betty said years later. "The war was hard on a lot of marriages."

As a result, *carpe diem* ruled. *Live it up tonight* was the dictum many followed during the war, married or not. While some of the men and women dealt with their loneliness with alcohol, many others coped by having affairs.

Betty and her husband spent a few days together on leave when Betty was stationed in Delhi. But the war had changed her. She had always been self-reliant, but living abroad and being able to call her own shots without having to first clear it with a male higher-up had only cemented her independent streak. During the weekend she spent with Alex, she often felt like she was talking to a stranger.

Their marriage was dissolving, and she knew it. And judging from his future plans—he told her he wanted to live in Thailand after the war and start an English-language newspaper—he knew it, too.

Besides, she had already fallen in love with another man, Colonel Richard Heppner. She had first met her newly appointed commanding officer back in Washington at OSS headquarters; Heppner had worked at Donovan's law firm before coming on board at the OSS from its early days. Before being assigned to the Kunming office, Heppner had worked in Special Operations in the London office and was well respected by enlisted and civilians alike. In China, he sat in on the MO morning planning sessions and first took an interest in Betty's work . . . and then in her.

Soon they were spending all their free time together, mostly going on long walks with his dog, Sammy, who would also steal away to Betty's desk during the day, providing Heppner with another excuse to spend time with her.

* * *

Despite her burgeoning relationship with Heppner, the MO Blues had started to hit Betty hard in Kunming. "I felt frustrated, brought on by an unfulfilled desire to tabulate results," she said. Over several months of work in China, she and her team had distributed more than two million leaflets, pamphlets, and other black propaganda to numerous units in the field, but she didn't see any discernable results. And the war was still deeply entrenched.

However, she did admit that compared to those working in the field, she had it relatively easy. "We didn't go out and sleep in the mud and blow up bridges," she said.

But she did take her fair share of trips on rickety prop planes to other OSS bases throughout China. In July 1945, Lieutenant Laird Nagel—who had worked with Zuzka on several MO assignments in Italy—came up with an idea for an MO project that he felt needed a woman's touch. He was based in Chongqing, and he thought Betty would be perfect for the job. Always game for an adventure, she flew to the MO base where he spelled out his idea, which involved the "comfort women" who were forced into sexual slavery by the Japanese military during the war. Most of the women had come from Korea and China and were usually based in one area, though they were occasionally moved into other regions during the war years.

Lieutenant Nagel called Betty because the Chinese army had rescued a group of Korean comfort women and thought that a story about one of the women, maybe in the form of a diary, would be just the thing to drive a wedge between Japanese officers and enlisted men.

"Split the officers and men," he told her. "Tell how officers pay her to spy on enlisted men, and that the brass confides in her that the war is nearly over, while the men in the ranks are going to be left behind in China as sacrificial goats."

Betty thought it was worth a shot. She headed for the hospital with an interpreter to interview some of the women. She wanted sob stories, but the women weren't at all interested in confiding in her. "All they seemed to be interested in was cadging cigarettes and lipsticks from the nurses," said Betty.

She was, however, a bit taken aback when one of the women wanted to know how much Betty made as a "comfort woman."

* * *

When Betty made her trip to visit the comfort women, the war had already been over in Europe for two months. With war still raging in the Far East, military planners were predicting that the Allied war with Japan would continue at least through the end of the year.

During one of Jane's last weekly Rumor Mill sessions before it was discontinued, one idea in particular stood out, that the Allies were planning to attack Hong Kong. She figured that such a rumor could potentially divert Japanese troops away from Japan, which would make the already weakened country much more vulnerable to attack. Jane okayed it and sent it in the next transmission, which landed on Betty's desk in Kunming a few days later.

Betty thought it could work. She typed up a radio script and handed it to the translator for the lead story for that afternoon's newscast. A few days later, reports from OSS agents in the field began to appear confirming that a large mass of Japanese troops was indeed heading toward Hong Kong.

At last! Some tangible results.

Since she'd started writing for black radio in China, Betty discovered she had a real knack for it. She particularly liked working with "the Seer," a Chinese announcer working for the OSS who provided astrological predictions during his nightly show. One night in late July 1945, Betty was hashing out ideas for future shows with one of her coworkers, who asked her to come up with something that would prove highly distressing to both the Chinese and Japanese.

What about an earthquake? Her team nixed it since earthquakes were pretty common in both countries.

A tidal wave? Again, thumbs-down. No problem, she'd come up with something.

She headed for her desk and thought back to Jane's rumor and how effective the mere threat of an attack had been against the Japanese. She figured that she didn't have to get any more specific; just suggesting the possibility of total destruction would be enough. Betty typed out a news report and handed it to the translator, who then forwarded it to the Seer.

On the evening of August 5, 1945, the Seer opened his show in a somber tone. "Something terrible is going to happen to Japan," he intoned. "We have checked the stars and there is something we can't even mention because it is so dreadful, and it is going to eradicate one whole area of Japan."

The next morning, the Allies dropped the atom bomb on Hiroshima.

* * *

Three days later, when Japanese surrender was not forthcoming, the Allies dropped a second atomic bomb on Nagasaki. This time the Japanese surrendered. The war was finally over.

When the OSS later heard about the Seer's broadcast the night before Hiroshima, they feared a leak from within, although by this time, of course, it was of little consequence. But the next time Colonel Heppner saw Betty, he pulled her aside and asked, "How in the world did you find out about this?"

"We just made it up," she replied. "The weird truth about MO is that if you make up incredible stories, sometimes they'll turn out to be true."

ACT FOUR

BACK TO
REALITY

Chapter 13

Zuzka

After Zuzka was discharged from the Army, she was immediately hired by the Office of War Information and sent to Salzburg, Austria, due to her fluency in German. Because there was no longer a need for wartime propaganda, the agency's priorities shifted to rebuilding devastated regions of Europe. In addition to repairing infrastructure and carting away the rubble from bombed buildings, a few staff members believed that part of the reconstruction effort—and celebration of the war's end—should include relaunching arts and culture events like the Salzburg Festival, a longtime summer music and theater event that had last been held in 1938.

Zuzka was put in charge of the festival and had just six weeks to single-handedly find musicians, singers, and conductors to perform at the event, which was scheduled for late August. Given the spottiness of phone lines and iffy mail delivery due to bombed-out infrastructure, she hit the road to visit musicians and make her case in person.

"The first two weeks I was on the road nonstop," she said. She traveled to Switzerland to meet with a conductor and then to Innsbruck to hire a soprano. She even convinced the Vienna Boys Choir to make an appearance. While the musicians were heartened by the prospect of work so soon after the end of hostilities, they were rightly skeptical about the availability of adequate lodging and food in Salzburg, which was far from guaranteed. So Zuzka used the Army uniform she'd held on to after her discharge to visit military bases at night where she could obtain food and supplies. "I helped 'liberate' canned food and cigarettes to be used in bartering for other foodstuffs that were only available on the black market," she said. This was the only way to guarantee that she could feed the artists.

Between meeting with musicians and stealing food from military commissaries, she called in favors from higher-ups who could help. But she also wanted to find time to make a quick side trip to Czechoslovakia to find out what was left of her family. One day in early July, everything came together, and she managed to hitch a ride to Brno with a Czech officer who was heading that way, as long as she could provide the gas.

After arranging for a weeklong leave and rounding up ten cans filled with gas, she headed to Brno with the Czech officer and an American soldier tagging along.

Once they crossed the border into her native country, Zuzka fell silent. "The landscape looked strangely different," she remembered years later. "The roads were in total disrepair, almost impassable with detours galore, and entire communities were totally deserted and the shutters on the houses were closed. There was no sign of life, human or animal."

After hours on the road, they decided to stop for the night in the town of Nemecky Brod, about one hundred kilometers from Brno. They found an inn and tavern packed with soldiers who were still celebrating the end of the war. The tavern was so smoky she couldn't see her hand in front of her face. Zuzka went in to negotiate for a room and a safe place to hide the jeep, a particularly valuable commodity. She booked a room, and her military escorts tucked the jeep into a shed; they'd spend the night in the vehicle.

Up in the room, she was so exhausted that even the carousing in the tavern couldn't keep her awake. Zuzka pulled a blanket off the bed only to encounter so many bedbugs that she could barely see the pillow. She pulled a chair to the middle of the room, took the container of DDT that was standard Army issue, and sprinkled enough of the poison to create a barrier around the chair. She sat down, crossed her arms, and promptly fell asleep.

At one point, she woke with a start to see the Czech officer who had accompanied her in the jeep standing in front of her, buck naked.

"The expression on his face and his area below the waistline was self-explanatory," she quipped years later. But she had vast experience interviewing and negotiating with surly German POWs; she knew how to handle the officer. "Look," she said, "if I start screaming now, it will end poorly for you as well as for me. So put a lid on, and tonight you will be in Bratislava with your wife."

Taken aback by Zuzka's directness, he apologized and left the room. The next morning, she mostly ignored the men as they passed through bombed-out villages. Not long after they crossed into Brno, Zuzka spotted a woman on the road who looked familiar.

Zuzka shouted at the driver to stop, but she jumped out of the jeep while it was still moving. "Mother!" she screamed.

The woman stopped and dropped the water jug she was carrying when she saw it was her own daughter. They embraced each other, screaming and crying, and the same thing happened a few minutes later when her father saw her for the first time in years. They both had thought Zuzka was dead, and vice versa.

She grabbed her bag from the jeep, and they headed toward what was left of her childhood home. "The roof was gone, there's a big hole right where my room used to be, and it was raining in the kitchen," she said. "But it was still standing."

Her parents told her that the house had been shelled by both Russians and Germans, and they updated her on how the family had fared through the war. Both parents had hid out in a different house in Brno before her father, Karel—a Jew—was captured in the fall of 1944 and sent to Theresienstadt, a notorious labor camp near Prague, while Olga stayed in Brno for the rest of the war. "My father came home from camp 40 pounds lighter and a very old man," Zuzka remembered. Her younger brother—also named Karel—had spent the war at Kleinstein, a concentration camp for Czechs who were half Jewish, and from his stories he'd gotten off relatively lightly. Her uncle didn't fare as well; he was imprisoned in Theresienstadt along with her father but was gassed just two days before the Russians liberated the camp.

Zuzka was very much relieved to discover that her immediate family had survived the war, but after spending just a week in her native land, she no longer felt like Czechoslovakia was home, and it wasn't just because of the destruction. When she first set foot on Czech soil again, she expected to be drawn into the old customs and culture. Rather, the trip reinforced her feelings that she was an American through and through.

"I was touched to see all the old things and places, but I looked at them from far away and there was nothing that could bring my 1939 world back into focus," she said. "I'm glad I went home, otherwise I would have kept wondering where I really belong. The old Zuzka is back there in Brno; the new one is scarcely related to her. The problem is now solved: I'm an American."

* * *

After a week in Brno, she hitched a ride back to Salzburg and resumed her work on bringing the festival to life. According to *Time* magazine, the event was a roaring success despite the acute limitations on venue, performers, and organizers.

"Last week the Salzburg Festival was on again—under the wary eye of the American Military Government," reported an article in the magazine. "White-helmet-ed MPs directed generals' limousines through cobbled streets. Inside the *Festspielhaus* some 50 hand-picked Austrians in dowdy evening clothes, were carefully segregated from U.S. soldiers who filled two-thirds of the auditorium. Then the

Mozarteum Orchestra, including 27 musicians ousted by the Nazis, played Mozart, Lehar and Johann Strauss.

"The only opera on this year's program is Mozart's *Il Seraglio*; it is the only one that the Salzburgers could fit out a complete set of scenery."

Once the festival was over, Zuzka had to pivot. She had two choices: She could stay in Austria and continue to work with the Office of War Information unit for a couple more years, or she could fly back to the US immediately.

Perhaps the epiphany she experienced in her birthplace cemented her decision, but she opted to return to the States, even though she had no idea what she'd do. It wasn't a big deal; after all, she'd always excelled at thinking on her feet, but she also had another good reason for being back on American soil:

Zuzka was pregnant, and she wanted her child to be born in America.

Her divorce was in process, and she hadn't seen her soon-to-be-ex-husband in years. Like Betty and many of her coworkers, she had been desperately lonely during the war—and after—and she sometimes craved more than just friendship.

After a plane, a truck, and a ship, she landed in Boston. Someone handed her a glass of milk, the first she'd had in years that wasn't powdered and reconstituted. Years later, she would refer to it as "nectar." Then she hopped on a train to New York, which she felt held more opportunities than Boston, and besides, it was somewhat familiar and already had a Czech community that she could fall into.

Zuzka felt very disconnected when she got off the train, and the multitudes of happy families reconnecting on the platform only underscored her loneliness. "There was no one waiting for me in New York," she said. "In fact, there was no one waiting for me anywhere in the U.S."

She was an unemployed veteran in the so-called 52–20 Club: For fifty-two weeks she'd receive twenty dollars a week for her military benefits.

Zuzka headed out of the train station and into the bustling city. She had no idea of her next move.

* * *

She reconnected with the local Czech community, which allowed her to cobble together a modest living. She took up a couple of law projects, translated a novel, and moved in with her former MO colleague, cartoonist Saul Steinberg, who was living in Greenwich Village after he left the military.

On June 1, 1946, her daughter, Marina, was born. Zuzka often referred to her as "a souvenir from Salzburg, a souvenir I am very happy about."

Some have speculated that the father was Major William Dewart, who she worked closely with at MO, but it was actually Lieutenant General Beverley Powell, who she had met while in Salzburg, and who was married with a wife and family back home in the States. In a letter to Powell after Marina was born, Zuzka described how she used a fake name for the father on the birth certificate—Ch. L. Lee—and if anyone asked, she told them he was a US officer who had been killed in a car crash shortly after the war was over. They both wanted to spare Powell and his family the stigma of an illegitimate birth. Besides, Zuzka felt she was perfectly capable of raising a child on her own. After all, her fierce independent streak had gotten her this far.

Ten days after giving birth, Zuzka landed a job at Voice of America, a radio broadcast service founded by the Office of War Information in 1942 as a way to broadcast news and information to occupied countries during the war. In 1945, it was taken over by the US State Department and continued to beam programs into countries that were grappling with the postwar world . . . which was all of them. Zuzka worked as both a writer and announcer on a daily twenty-minute Czech broadcast. Sometimes her babysitter was a no-show and she had no choice but to bring Marina to the studio with her.

Occasionally, coworkers at the Polish and Bulgarian VOA stations cared for Marina while Zuzka taped her broadcast.

She was able to pay a few bills, but life as a single mother in post-war New York was a tough one. Her parents had begged her to return to Czechoslovakia, and though she was an American through and through—as was her daughter—in her homeland at least she'd have reliable childcare.

In May 1947, when Marina was almost a year old, they got on a plane and headed to Brno. Once they settled in, Zuzka's babysitting problem was instantly solved, but despite her military experience, language fluency, and law degree, she couldn't find a job. At the time, a Communist takeover of the country was brewing, and Zuzka was clearly an undesirable. "We can't hire you," they'd tell her, "you served in the wrong army."

A few months later, an old friend was very surprised to see her in town. "What the hell are you doing here?" he asked with alarm. "This whole thing is going to collapse any day. Get out as soon as you can with your child." He told her she was in great danger, not only because she had been in the US Army but especially because she had worked for the OSS. "They'll arrest you," he warned, "maybe even execute you."

Zuzka took his warnings seriously, and on the last day of 1947, she and Marina took a train to Prague and flew back to the United States.

With the help of the Soviet Union, the Communists took over the Czechoslovak government in February 1948.

They got out just in time.

* * *

Zuzka and Marina returned to New York, but struggled even more than before. Women weren't welcome at many jobs since all of the good ones were being snapped up by returning male veterans; women were expected to return to their prewar lives of keeping house, having babies, and taking care of their husbands. As the culture turned more socially conservative, and many Americans reverted to traditional gender roles, single mothers were not welcomed with open arms.

Zuzka thought she might have better luck in Washington, so they picked up again and moved to DC, where Zuzka quickly landed work as a dental assistant. Her former boss at the Czech embassy took her and Marina in as boarders, and Zuzka was able to relax . . . a little. She had room, board, and built-in babysitters in the several other young women who lived there.

Zuzka soon left the dentist's office to become a research analyst at the Library of Congress, a job she would hold for twenty years, and where she would meet a Polish aristocrat named Joseph Junosza Podoski, also a research analyst. They were soon inseparable outside the office, and Zuzka proved that her facility for languages hadn't left her when she soon became fluent in Polish. They married in 1954 and continued to work at the Library until 1968, when they both retired.

They headed to Europe to celebrate their retirement and started out in Vienna, and they both fell in love with the city. "I went to Vienna for a few days and got stuck there for nine years," she said years later. She loved being in Austria again and took a job in the Vienna office of the American Fund for Czechoslovak Refugees. They finally returned to Washington in 1977, and she retired again. This time it stuck.

When her husband died in 1984, Zuzka coped by immersing herself in a small but vibrant group of Czechs in the nation's capital. She especially loved to knit and make crafts for the Christmas bazaars held at local Czech churches. She also became a regular at the Czech embassy, where she became a kind of mother hen to some of the younger employees, which extended to washing and ironing their shirts. She was often invited to parties and events at the embassy, and she always made sure to wear her Army uniform, the Bronze Star prominently pinned to her lapel.

She also became involved in events and gatherings held by other former OSS veterans. In October 1991, she attended a commemorative banquet for retired OSS personnel and ended up sitting at the same table as Betty. They had previously met at other OSS events, and quickly began to catch up. But Zuzka couldn't help but notice the man sitting next to Betty, who she introduced as Joseph Randolph Coolidge IV, a recent widower. He had served in an R&A mapping unit in North Africa and the Far East and, like Zuzka, had a Bronze Star, along with a Purple Heart. They began comparing notes and the spark between them was immediate. They soon became inseparable and split their time between his apartment in New York, her condo in DC, and a small cabin on Squam Lake in New Hampshire.

When he died in 1999, Zuzka was heartbroken. "For seven years and nine months we had the most wonderful relationship one can hope for," she said.

She moved back to Washington full-time, where she lived another ten years. She died of cardiovascular disease on August 16, 2009, at the age of ninety-five and was buried in Arlington National Cemetery.

Though she lived a far-reaching life after the war, Zuzka never stopped being a soldier. At her funeral service, a friend eulogized her in this way:

"She always carried in her purse three objects: a knife, a spoon, and a handkerchief, the basic equipment every soldier carries as a reminder of war."

Chapter 14

Marlene

With the war officially over, the clandestine radio broadcasts ended and the USO tours were disbanded. Marlene's boys were finally going home, and so was she.

Just like Zuzka, before Marlene returned to the States, she wanted to visit her homeland to see if her family had survived the war. First, she located her sister, Elisabeth, and her husband. For all the years of the war, Marlene had imagined that they had suffered incredible hardships. But instead, she discovered, they actually operated a small theater for the Nazis who ran the Bergen-Belsen concentration camp. Marlene was horrified, and cut off all contact with them from that day forward; for the rest of her life, she would deny ever having a sister.

Next, she looked for her mother, Josefine, who had been living in Berlin before the war. Marlene was overjoyed when she found that she was still alive, though extremely frail. She unfortunately died a couple of months later.

Marlene returned to the States heartbroken at the loss of her mother, and uncertain of what came next.

* * *

She landed in the US on July 13, 1945, and almost immediately began pining for her former life in the Army.

"Coming home from the war was an interesting experience for my mother because suddenly everything was mundane," said Maria Riva. "They took away the guns that the boys had given her, and suddenly she didn't have a uniform to wear. She had to think about hats and stockings, and she hated this. She also had to earn a living. It was a very difficult time for her."

But most of all, she missed her boys, and doing something she really believed in. Like Betty and so many others who returned from overseas, it took her a long time to stop referring to the war in the present tense.

"It's cold back here in civilian life," Marlene said. "Over there, everybody was so friendly and cordial. Why does it take the nearness of death to make people become alive?"

Marlene soon returned to Europe, settling in Paris to entertain the American soldiers who were part of the occupation forces. But she needed money, and the Presidential Medal of Freedom and French Legion of Honor accolades she received for her wartime service wouldn't pay the bills. So even though she had announced that she was done with making movies a year earlier, she signed on to costar in *Martin Roumagnac*, a French film, to replenish her coffers, and others followed.

She decided to return to her cabaret roots and developed an act for a show in Las Vegas, mostly because she discovered that the money was so much better than what the movies paid. She soon took the show on tour all over the world.

As a result of her newfound popularity, Marlene signed with Columbia Records in 1951. The label had approached her to produce a live album based on the strength of the audiences for her cabaret act.

Mitch Miller, who would later become famous for telling TV viewers to "follow the bouncing ball" on his hit TV show *Sing Along with Mitch*, was working as the director of artists and repertoire for Columbia Records when Marlene came on board. She brought the masters of the songs she had sung for Morale Operations to one of their early meetings and played them for him. She thought that perhaps some of the twelve songs could be re-released as a new album.

Miller loved her idea, but said that the songs would have to be newly recorded in order to make the best album possible.

"Never," Marlene replied. "I will never feel that way again."

Miller acknowledged that there was some truth to that. But he told her that new recordings would be even better since the technology had improved considerably since her wartime sessions, when recording studios were hampered by equipment shortages and cobbled-together repairs. Plus, new recordings would be enhanced by the fact that she could now take her time with each song; after all, her 1944 sessions were absolute pressure cookers, requiring her to produce four songs ready for air in each three-hour session.

"I talked to her about breathing and the conscious things she could do with it," said Miller. "She could concentrate on the artistic, rather than the 'historical' value of what she was doing."

After thinking it over, Marlene agreed to re-record her songs. And getting permission to reproduce the masters no longer mattered.

* * *

Marlene Dietrich Overseas was a hit and appeared near the top of the music charts all across the country. Miller decided to capitalize on the album's success and paired her with another one of the label's singers, up-and-comer Rosemary Clooney—aunt of actor George Clooney, who was another nine years away from being born—who was celebrating her first big hit with "Come On-a My House."

They teamed up to sing four songs to be issued on *Rosie and Marlene*, an EP disc that came out in late 1953. The band was led by Jimmy Carroll, who had conducted the orchestra for the original OSS sessions and for the re-recorded version. Among the songs was "Too Old to Cut the Mustard," a novelty song about the challenges of dealing with an older man. Against all odds, the song hit Top 40

a few jokes while wearing a skin-tight sequined dress that left little to the imagination. Many critics were dumbfounded at her success.

"People will pay to see her regardless of her act—an act in which she sings badly because her tremulous voice lacks timbre and range, and which she dances inadequately," wrote columnist Lloyd Shearer. "Yet Marlene is always a sellout. How does she do it?"

Money. Lots of it. "Let's not fool anyone," she told him. "It takes money to be glamorous nowadays, and glamour is what I sell in my act, and it costs plenty."

Her dress cost $12,000. And she had two of them. She also maintained that performing in nightclubs stretched her acting chops much more than on a movie set.

"I had no desire to be a film actress, to always play somebody else, to be always beautiful with somebody constantly straightening out your every eyelash," she said. "I never see myself as an actress on the screen. But when I sing my songs, *then* I am an actress. I act the lyrics."

Plus, onstage *she* was in control, just as she had been in charge on the USO tour and while recording the MO songs. "I can choose my own songs and my own scripts," she said. "I don't have to creep into someone else's character as in the movies."

Singing brought her back to her early years in Weimar and Berlin, yes, but more importantly, it brought her back to World War II, which she considered to be the best years of her life. But she was getting tired of the masquerade and the hours it took to put herself together for a brief forty-five-minute foray onstage, not to mention the exhaustion from traveling all over the world. In just one month in early 1968, Marlene performed shows in Israel, Australia, Paris, and New York. "It's getting more difficult to be happy," she admitted.

In 1973, she decided to try something different and bring her one-woman show to TV. After all, it was hard to refuse when she would be paid $250,000 to sing fourteen songs. But it was a big mistake. "I always said I would never appear on TV unless Orson Welles directed, but he was too expensive and everything went wrong," she complained. First the lighting director used orange lights during "La Vie en Rose." Then there were the endless commercials during the show, where Kraft was the primary sponsor. "Every two minutes, somebody is talking about cheese," she complained. "How many cheeses can you sell in one hour?"

The technical staff added a laugh track to the show, which Marlene detested, and deleted the songs that were not in English. At the press conference, the journalists "asked me the most stupid questions of all time, like if I like long skirts or short skirts."

It was almost the last straw.

* * *

Marlene unexpectedly made her last public appearance on September 29, 1975, during a performance in Sydney, Australia, when she fell off the stage and broke her leg. She returned to Paris to convalesce, and she was still recovering when her husband died on June 24, 1976. It all proved to be too much for her, and sometime in the early 1980s, she decided she'd had enough. She took to her bed in a small apartment in the 8th Arrondissement . . . and never left.

"It's so hard to be a living legend, always looking like people expect, always thirty years old, never disappointing the audience," said Maria Riva. "Always the wig and the makeup and the body, that's so much. She saw it as her duty to be perfect [in public] and she was just tired of the effort."

Before Marlene Dietrich died on May 6, 1992, she had often made a point of saying that the work she did during the war years was "the most important work I've ever done." But it was also the most important thing she had ever done for *herself*.

"It was the best role she ever played," said Maria Riva. "She earned laurels for her heroic courage, collected medals, and was honored and respected. The officer's daughter had found her true calling, she was playing the part of the brave soldier."

Chapter 15

Betty

The war was over and people all over the world were celebrating . . .
    . . . But not Betty.

"I started to drink the lemon powder, sugar, and vodka highball someone thrust into my hand thinking that this was what people did when wars were won," said Betty. But she had no desire to celebrate.

She knew it sounded horrible, that she was sad that the war had ended. "I was glad, like everyone else that it was over, because the people who might've been killed tomorrow would be alive now for the rest of their natural lives," she said. "But there was a sudden vacuum which peace had brought. Up to now there had been purpose, urgency, importance in what we were doing."

"Suddenly, we had no direction, and the prospect of returning to a routine life was difficult to imagine," she said.

She was also surprised to find herself questioning the role that she had played in pitting one side against the other.

"Did I hate the Germans? The Japanese? Not really. I helped make up the slogans to make the other people hate," she said. "Packaged hate, like packaged breakfast foods, produced by the ad man in uniform. And a prize of a promise in every package—the corner drugstore, ice cubes, America."

She was at a total loss. But her depression lifted minutes later when a jeep rolled by with Richard Heppner in the back seat. She hopped in, instantly cheered by being with the man she loved, and what he told her next lifted her spirits even more.

The war might have ended, but there were a lot of loose ends to tie up in the aftermath. For one, it was the responsibility of the OSS to send cease-fire messages to troops in the field and to inform them of their next mission: to head to POW camps throughout China to free Allied prisoners of war.

Betty became a liaison between Heppner and the communications office responsible for getting the word out to the field units, as well as helping to arrange medics to tag along. "It was probably the best thing that could've happened to me because the war made a far more graceful exit for my life," she said. She was performing a vital task and felt useful once again.

Some of the other MO staffers also stayed on in Kunming to help with the transition out of war, and by September, they were starting to head back to the States. By then, Betty felt a little more mentally prepared to head back, but Donovan offered her the chance to stay in China for an extra couple of months so she could write the official history of OSS in China. She accepted the assignment and moved to a temporary office in Shanghai, where she settled into work.

By the time she stepped onto a plane to head back to the States on October 23, she was finally ready.

But she had her first taste of culture shock—and the realization that the autonomy and independence that she had experienced for the last three years was over. On active duty in a war zone, life was too frenzied—and precious—to worry about what other people—particularly men—thought of you.

In Delhi, Calcutta, and Kunming, it didn't much matter. As long as a woman could do the job, her male coworkers were just fine, respecting Betty's work and that of the other women. "I had enough experience in journalism to figure out what would make a good story and how to twist it that they listened to me," she said. "I had no trouble at all, and none of the women working with me did either."

But now, upon reentry into a world that at its core probably hadn't changed that much, all of her defenses were suddenly rising to the surface. Returning to the United States after living overseas was almost more than she could bear.

She greeted a guard after landing in Cairo on the first leg of the trip home and immediately started second-guessing herself. "I smiled at the man and said hi, hating myself the next second for being a patronizing, fatuous female who's been overseas too long in the land where the ratio was twenty men to one white woman," she said. "Why do we consciously appoint ourselves representatives of the pure unadulterated institution of the American girl? And why did all the girls at home imagine themselves the symbol of what the men were fighting to come home to?"

She knew she was overthinking it, but she couldn't help herself.

After Cairo came Casablanca, then the Azores, where she paged through a copy of *The New York Times* dated the previous day. One more stop—Bermuda—and then she'd be at her final destination of Washington.

If she hoped her annoyance would fade as she got closer to home, she was disappointed. When she arrived at Union Station, she seethed at the scene. But just like Zuzka felt when she first landed in New York after a couple of hard years away at war, Betty, with her war-weary eyes, thought it looked as though nothing had changed. "People in the waiting room were casual and complacent, like stage props," she said. "A sailor with his duffel bag and his girl asleep with her head on his lap, an old lady in prim black suit and bird nest hat. I was vaguely annoyed. Had the nation even absorbed the full emotional impact of war?"

Housing in Washington was still hard to come by, and her aunt's house was still crammed to the rafters with boarders. Betty had heard about several OSS returnees who were renting a yacht that was moored on the Potomac. There was one tiny room available—would she like it?

She moved in, and her aggravation eased slightly. At least she'd be living with like-minded people who understood her mixed feelings about the end of the war, which included the necessity to return to some degree of autonomy in everyday life.

"During the war we made absolutely no decisions, they were all made for you and you did as you were told," she said. "The OSS was like a big family where we all lived together, ate all our meals together, and traveled together, which was not a normal way of living for an adult."

Being in Washington also made her uncomfortable as Betty associated it with a previous life that no longer existed, and one she had no desire to return to. With her marriage definitely over, she was waiting to hear from Heppner, who was still stationed overseas. She missed him terribly. "I was in love and we didn't know what we were going to do," she said.

She was stuck in limbo, so she booked a flight home to Hawaii, where at least she could be with her family while she waited to hear from him. While she was in Honolulu, she wrote several articles for the *Star-Bulletin*, her old newspaper. It was better than sitting around doing nothing.

* * *

Two months later, her life had turned around for the better. Betty was living on the Upper West Side of Manhattan, and her personal life had vastly improved. Heppner had also moved to New York to work with Donovan, who had returned to the city to work at his law firm. Betty and Heppner saw each other regularly while they waited for their divorces to become final.

In early 1946, Betty took a job at *Glamour* magazine, writing about fake furs and shoes and designers, but she didn't last a year. "Discussing fashion after all I'd done seemed absolutely ridiculous," she admitted.

After she quit, Betty started writing a book about her years in the OSS for the Macmillan Company, a New York publisher; *Undercover Girl* was published on October 26, 1947, and was featured by the Literary Guild and Book of the Month clubs. General Donovan wrote the introduction.

Sales were brisk, and the reviews were generally positive. One of her previous coworkers raved. "It is a revelation of what we didn't know about Elizabeth," wrote journalist Peter Edson. "Oh, the skull-duggery that sweet little girl was capable of."

The New York Times reviewed the book on two separate occasions. "Mrs. MacDonald's account of life among the whispering thousands of OSS tyros in Washington is irreverent and entertaining," wrote critic Orville Prescott. And the University of Washington, her alma mater, added *Undercover Girl* as a required textbook in their courses on psychological warfare.

Betty and Richard married on July 3, 1948, at her grandmother's house in Clinton, Connecticut. After a short honeymoon with stops in Sea Island, Georgia, and Greenbrier in West Virginia, they moved into an apartment at 360 First Avenue in Manhattan.

After a few years in New York, they moved to Alexandria, Virginia; now that Betty was happily married, the city didn't feel as alien to her as before. Richard was working at the Pentagon as deputy assistant secretary of defense for International Security Affairs, and Betty got a job with Voice of America, like Zuzka. She programmed the shows and wrote news stories, though at times she found it difficult. "After spending three years in MO disguising the truth, selecting stories and developing rumors, I had great difficulty writing a straight news story," she admitted.

In her spare time, she volunteered with the Girl Scouts and started writing a children's book about a seeing-eye dog named Inky, which was published in 1957.

She was the happiest she'd ever been.

And then, on May 14, 1958, disaster struck when her forty-nine-year-old husband died suddenly of a burst aorta.

Betty had managed to pull herself together several times before in her life, but Richard's unexpected death absolutely paralyzed her. She had another children's book, *Palace Under the Sea*, scheduled for publication in January 1959, and she was able to complete the last-minute prepublication tasks in the immediate aftermath of losing her husband.

But she couldn't escape from her deep depression. Several friends from her MO days had signed on to work for the CIA, which had become the successor to the OSS, and they thought that going back to work was the best thing she could do under the circumstances.

Shortly after *Palace Under the Sea* was published, she met with Allen Dulles, the head of the spy agency, who asked if she wanted to work for the CIA in MO-related operations in Tokyo, and she immediately agreed. Dulles pulled some strings to have *Palace* translated into Japanese, and the book and subsequent tour through the country became Betty's cover story.

During her time in Japan, she met Frederick Ballard McIntosh, a fighter pilot and lieutenant colonel in the Air Force. They famously hit it off and married on May 26, 1962. The following year, he retired from the service and they returned to the States, settling in Leesburg, Virginia; Frederick went on to have a storied career as a dowser, and Betty retired from the CIA in 1973. When he died in 2004 after forty-two years of marriage, she moved into a nearby retirement community, where she died at the age of one hundred on June 8, 2015.

Betty had crammed a lot of living into her century of life. But like Zuzka, Jane, and Marlene, her war service was the highlight. "There was a real reason for what we were doing in those days," she said. "A lot of the things we tried didn't work, but it was war, and it was important."

"Never again would I feel so alive, so completely engaged in something I knew would never come around again," said Betty.

Chapter 16

Jane

Jane remained in Washington after the war. After all, Henri planned to stay on in the military to help supervise the postwar occupation in Tokyo as a liaison officer on General Douglas MacArthur's staff.

One of her husband's first postwar duties was to attend the official Japanese surrender ceremony on board the USS *Missouri* on the morning of September 2, 1945, less than a month after the Allied bombing of the Japanese cities of Hiroshima and Nagasaki. Before signing the documents, MacArthur spoke for five minutes about the restoration of peace and the need for freedom, tolerance, and justice no matter which side you were on during the war.

Back in Washington, with nothing to occupy her time—and no one to fight—Jane felt a little lost, just like Betty, Zuzka, and Marlene. That changed when she discovered she was pregnant again. She gave birth to a daughter in February 1946, and her days were soon busy again, especially since Marcia was born blind.

In May 1946, Henri left Tokyo to return to Washington to await his next orders, and he met his daughter for the first time. Jane was overjoyed to see her husband again, but she didn't expect him to stay long since he was appointed to be commander of the USS *Little Rock*. Indeed, he was home just a month before he left for the ship, which was then stationed in European waters.

He could have continued on in the military, but he and Jane had had enough of life apart for months on end. Henri was given the option of becoming naval attaché at the American embassy in either France or Germany, the same position he'd held in Tokyo. He opted for France as French was one of the nine languages he spoke (German wasn't). Jane was thrilled, both to be reunited with her husband and to live in France, though French was never her strong suit.

The family left for Paris on May 6, 1947; Cynthia was now thirteen, and Marcia had just turned one. But after more than five years of war, Paris wasn't in much better shape than Tokyo. The city was impassable in many places; apartment buildings and homes were in disrepair and often uninhabitable. Most buildings in the city had gone unheated for the length of the war, except for those that had been occupied by the Germans.

When Jane first laid eyes on the three-story stone house that would become their home at 64 Boulevard Suchet, she burst into tears. "During the war, the Germans had used it as a radio station, the Americans later used it as a photo lab, and both had treated the house badly," said Henri years later. "We borrowed cots and a few pieces of furniture until our furniture came from the US."

Jane and Henri began arranging for repairs to the house, but supplies as well as contractors to do the work were difficult to source. "We learned how impoverished France had been by the war," he said. "Paint, brushes, lumber, nails, in fact any kind of repair materials were almost impossible to find." Little by little, through diplomatic connections and sheer luck, Jane was able to transform the house into a home, as well as a place suitable for entertaining embassy guests.

Along with building supplies, food was also strictly rationed. Flour, meat, milk, and sugar were in extremely short supply along with gasoline and clothing. Of course Jane had gone down this road before in Tokyo, but she was tired of scouring empty shelves and searching out black markets. "It was not easy to live in Paris in 1947," said Henri. Fortunately, the State Department set up a commissary where staff and their families could buy food and other supplies more readily.

Between fixing up the house and caring for her children, Jane's days were full, but she still wanted to do more, something of an artistic bent for a change. Back in Tokyo, she had taken classes in *ikebana*, the art of Japanese flower arranging, and she started working with flowers in France, first to spruce up the house and for embassy events, and then to teach classes in the art form.

She also did her part to help the embassy run smoothly, at least the entertaining aspect of it. The previous attaché had always preferred to entertain at home instead of in a nearby restaurant or other establishment, many of which, in any case, had been destroyed during the war, and those that survived reopened with limited menus due to strict postwar rationing.

With the war over, many American VIPs and politicians were eager to travel overseas again on official business, and Paris was always at the top of their lists. They often needed help navigating around the city and finding essential products and services, and Jane often made recommendations for the wives of visiting dignitaries who wanted to see the best hairdresser or laundry facilities in the city. It was a far cry from her previous work in MO, but at least she felt useful.

Just as she had refused to hold her tongue with OSS officers who thought they knew better, Jane didn't hesitate to shun those visitors who didn't treat her with respect. When Field Marshal Bernard Law Montgomery, an officer with the British Army, visited the embassy, Jane pretty much avoided him. "Jane didn't care for him," Henri said years later. "She said that he was obviously not a feminist, and he didn't like to talk to women. If ladies approached him and he saw men near him, he would turn away and talk to the men."

Despite the limitations, Jane settled into postwar life in Paris as best she could. She took care of Marcia, and Cynthia became a student at the Catholic school at Marymount Convent in Paris. Gradually, the supply issues started to ease in the city, transportation became more regular, and the prices of everything began to drop. Jane also started to accompany Henri on his travels around Europe and to England, and they met with the Duke and Duchess of Windsor several times.

Jane and Henri entertained regularly at the embassy, and it wasn't unusual for them to receive several invitations each night for events at the other embassies in the city. "Our social life was very tiring," Henri said. "There were so many parties [and dinners] that we were invited to when we had no real desire to go, but felt we ought to put in an appearance. We were glad when we didn't have to go out every night and could stay at home quietly."

But it wasn't all parties at the embassy; trouble was starting to brew throughout France in 1949 in the form of resistance against the American presence in the country. Hand-painted signs saying "U.S. Go Home!" popped up on walls and bridges throughout the country as rumblings against the postwar American occupation in Paris increased. During the 1949 election, a quarter of French citizenry voted for the Communist Party. Henri and Jane were in Normandy on June 6, 1949, for the anniversary of the D-Day landings, and they returned home to find a hand grenade placed at the gate to their house.

They stayed at the embassy for three more years before Henri decided to retire from his position in June 1952; he had originally planned to stay in the job for only a few years. He and Jane pondered where to go next, but they had lived abroad for the majority of their married life and had made a good life and friends for themselves in Paris, so they decided to stay.

He didn't stay retired for long, however, and took a job as chief of the Paris bureau of Radio Free Europe. Since Jane was no longer required to entertain extensively or reluctantly attend cocktail parties at other embassies, she threw herself into a variety of volunteer jobs, from creating needlepoint covers for antique kneelers at the American Cathedral in Paris to helping out at their occasional rummage sales.

Because she knew firsthand the challenges of raising a blind child, she focused her efforts for organizations that helped the blind. The American Library in Paris had an active Department for the Blind, and Jane served as chairman of the Junior Guild Reading Project for the Blind for a few years. When the department director left, she stepped into that role on a volunteer basis.

This proved to be a good outlet for her prodigious energy. In the four years she held the position, she expanded services to people in eighteen different countries and recorded books for university students. Jane and Henri also hosted blind students from America in their home. In 1967, Steve Speicher, a sixteen-year-old blind musician from Indianapolis, stayed with Henri and Jane and relied on their contacts to visit their friends in other parts of France.

But by the late 1960s, life in France was becoming untenable for the family. In the spring of 1968, French universities were extremely overcrowded and struggling economically. Students tried to negotiate with administrators for better conditions, but the two groups couldn't agree on changes. Spurred on by the countercultural protests that were starting to catch on in the United States at the time, students at Nanterre University, located in a Paris suburb, protested over the education they were getting by holding regular rallies in the streets. Workers from factories and office buildings soon joined the students in support of their efforts. Their protests quickly turned to global issues, including the Vietnam War and fighting Yankee imperialism, which of course directly targeted Jane and her family. Riots broke out, and ten million employees throughout the country went on strike for improved working conditions and better pay, causing the French economy to grind to a halt.

In 1969, Jane and Henri returned to the United States, settling in Palo Alto, California. She quickly became involved in the Daughters of the American Revolution, joining the Los Altos chapter and eventually serving in several positions on the statewide level. She also traveled all over California giving talks and seminars at DAR meetings and luncheons. In one talk at a Santa Cruz luncheon, she spoke about the superiority of the French naval fleet over the British during the American Revolution, which resulted in the American victory at Yorktown.

When Henri died on April 4, 1977, Jane was bereft; they had been married for over forty years. But she decided to stay on in California and became even more involved in DAR activities, becoming state conference coordinator of programs and the state chairman of public relations in 1988.

In the 1990s, she decided to move back East, settling in Washington, DC, for a few years before moving in 1998 to a retirement community in Southern Pines, North Carolina, to be near a friend who lived there and who she had known when she lived in Washington in the 1940s.

Jane Smith-Hutton died on September 22, 2002, at the age of ninety-one. She was buried at Arlington National Cemetery beside her husband. Like the other women, her wartime activities proved to be a tough act to follow; despite the politics and hardships she faced at the OSS, she relished the freedom and independence the job provided.

She spent the rest of her life chasing that high.

ACKNOWLEDGMENTS

Propaganda Girls has been years in the making, and many patient folks have been along for the ride, including:

Scott Mendel of the Mendel Media Group, whose fortitude is legendary.

Hannah O'Grady and Madeline Alsup at St. Martin's Press, for steering *Propaganda Girls* through the editorial process.

Sim Smiley and Ann Trevor, for invaluable research assistance while digging in the dusty OSS archives in College Park, Maryland.

Katherine Breaks, for providing me with a copy of her thesis, "The Ladies of the OSS: The Apron Strings of Intelligence in World War II."

Charles Pinck of the OSS Society for photos and tips.

Sheila Schwartz at the Saul Steinberg Foundation, for providing photos of Zuzka in Rome.

Susan Seymour of Pitzer College, for helpful details on Cora Jacobs and the MO office in Ceylon.

Sarli Hermansky, Zuzka's niece, for helpful insight.

David W. Sinclair, for providing photos of his grandmother, Jane Smith-Hutton.

The late Cynthia Bowers and Marcia Smith-Hutton, Jane's daughters, who spoke with me about their mother's life before and after the OSS.

Newspapers.com, a veritable gold mine of articles that helped flesh out the lives of the four women.

Baker Library at Dartmouth College, whose databases provided access to countless additional archives.

Finally, Alex Ishii, who helps hold down the fort.

NOTES

INTRODUCTION

2   "if successful can be more effective": Elizabeth MacDonald, *Undercover Girl* (New York: Macmillan, 1947), vii–viii.

3   "Women seemed to have a feeling": Betty McIntosh, interview by Maochun Yu, OSS Oral History Project, May 2, 1997.

4   "Just look straight ahead": Barbara Lauwers Podoski, interview by Christof Mauch, OSS Oral History Project, September 4, 1996.

CHAPTER 1: BETTY

10   "We need to get down": Elizabeth P. McIntosh, interview by Leslie Sewell, Elizabeth P. McIntosh Collection [AFC/2001/001/30838], Veterans History Project, American Folklife Center, Library of Congress, 2001.

12   "I saw a rooftop": Elizabeth P. McIntosh, "Honolulu After Pearl Harbor: A Report Published for the First Time, 71 Years Later," *Washington Post*, December 6, 2012.

12   "shrapnel coursing through your chest": Ibid.

13   "Can you do something about that?": Bob Bergin, "Inside the OSS: An Interview with Elizabeth P. McIntosh," *WWII History*, July 2007, https://warfarehistorynetwork.com/article/an-interview-with-elizabeth-p-mcintosh/.

14   "Write something from the women's point of view": McIntosh, "Honolulu After Pearl Harbor."

14   "I couldn't figure out why": Ibid.
14   "I had never known that blood": Ibid.
15   "Their clothes were blue-black": Ibid.
16   "I think it would be too frightening": Ibid.
17   "And then I'd hide them": Christine Donnelly, "Elizabeth Peet '31 McIntosh," *Punahou Bulletin*, Fall 2011.
18   "what had gone on before": Ibid.
18   "we'd sit there and talk baseball": Ibid.
18   "she confronts irate teachers": Ibid.
19   "all kinds of people were coming": Bergin, "Inside the OSS," July 2007.
20   "I felt like we weren't getting anywhere": Elizabeth P. McIntosh, interview by Aaron-Paula Thompson, 2012 Virginia Women in History program, February 29, 2012, https://youtu.be/J_occuReLU4.
21   "and I wrote that up": Bergin, "Inside the OSS," July 2007.
22   "the print blouses with big bows": Betty MacDonald, "Cuffnotes," *Honolulu Star-Bulletin*, February 4, 1942.

CHAPTER 2: ZUZKA

25   "My father never did": Barbara Lauwers Podoski, interview, Women's Memorial Foundation Oral History Project, August 5, 2005.
26   "I was too squeamish": Ibid.
27   "You can add it to your tea": Ibid.
27   "He'll be able to taste": Ibid.
30   "Off with you to the embassy": Barbara Podoski, "Me Too," in *On All Fronts: Czechoslovaks in World War II*, ed. Lewis M. White (Boulder: East European Monographs, 1992), 217.
31   "And you will write it for me!": Ibid., 218.
31   "he put me down when my description": Ibid.
32   "I broke down crying": Ibid.
32   "There was a huge ado": Ibid.
32   "If he won't join the army": Ibid., 219.
33   "it would surely help": Ibid.
33   "I didn't want to spend years": Podoski, Women's Memorial Foundation, August 5, 2005.
33   "a great adventure": Podoski, "Me Too," 219.
33   "so in the Army": Podoski, Women's Memorial Foundation, August 5, 2005.

CHAPTER 3: JANE

41   "so we were careful not to discuss": Henri Smith-Hutton, *The Reminiscences of Captain Henri Smith-Hutton, US Navy (Retired)*, 2 vols., Naval Institute Oral History (Annapolis: US Naval Institute, 1976), 73.

42   "there is no more imported whiskey": H. O. Thompson, "Life of Foreigners in Japan Lacks Ease Once Associated with Residence in Far East," *Cedar Rapids Gazette*, July 31, 1941.

45   "I saw maimed, undernourished and mentally ill": Sergeant Donald Bishop, "From 'Prison' In Tokyo To Fort Bragg 'Haven,'" *Charlotte Observer*, September 20, 1942.

46   "Let's wake everyone up!": Max Hill, *Exchange Ship* (New York: Farrar & Rinehart, 1942), 84.

46   "Fortunately, she didn't catch them": Henri Smith-Hutton, *The Reminiscences*, 373.

47   "It would have made all of the Allies": Ibid., 381.

CHAPTER 4: MARLENE

49   "I shall probably never again": "Marlene Dietrich Shuns Reich Films," *New York Times*, September 21, 1933.

51   "but rather on what it had become": Guido Knopp, *Hitler's Women* (New York: Routledge, 2003), 265.

51   "I couldn't resist twisting the knife": Charles Higham, *Marlene: The Life of Marlene Dietrich* (New York: Norton, 1977), 1.

51   "taking from Dietrich the oath": Maria Riva, *Marlene Dietrich* (New York: Knopf, 1993), 478.

52   "the only goal was humble submission": Karin Wieland, *Dietrich & Riefenstahl: Hollywood, Berlin, and a Century in Two Lives* (New York: Liveright, 2015), 31.

52   "I wanted a name that was all mine": Ibid.

53   "I thought Marlene was": Ibid.

54   "Maybe soon a time will come": Ibid., 42

56   "The long, bloody war was over": Steven Bach, *Marlene Dietrich: Life and Legend* (New York: William Morrow, 1992), 66.

58   "These parties are nauseatingly boring": J. David Riva, ed., *A Woman at War: Marlene Dietrich Remembered* (Detroit: Wayne State University/Painted Turtle, 2006), 19.

58   "box office poison": Wieland, *Dietrich & Riefenstahl*, 247.

59   "From now on, you must not appear": Knopp, *Hitler's Women*, 300.

60 "to eliminate all wasteful use": "Women in Pants OK'd by Studios; Stars Drop Frills," *Variety*, April 15, 1942.

60 "That was my only desire": Knopp, *Hitler's Women*, 303–4.

60 "I couldn't do much": Charlotte Chandler, *Marlene: Marlene Dietrich, A Personal Biography* (New York: Simon & Schuster, 2011), 157.

CHAPTER 5: ZUZKA

63 "the other girls would just stare": Podoski, Women's Memorial Foundation, August 5, 2005.

63 "grab the fork in your right paw": Ibid.

63 "DF doesn't even know": Ibid.

63 "I thought it was sheer luxury": Podoski, OSS Oral History Project, September 4, 1996.

64 "And if anybody asks us": Russell Miller, *Behind the Lines: The Oral History of Special Operations in World War II* (New York: St. Martin's Press, 2002), 67.

64 "I'd identify the language": Podoski, OSS Oral History Project, September 4, 1996.

65 "Some were malicious": Ibid.

66 "eventually spring came": Ibid.

66 "We wrapped, but didn't get warm": Podoski, "Me Too," 221.

66 "flanked by three faces": Ibid., 222.

66 "Give a report in ten words or less": Ibid.

67 "thanks to the languages": Podoski, OSS Oral History Project, September 4, 1996.

67 "I broke my collarbone": Podoski, "Me Too," 222.

67 "We were supposed to supply": Podoski, OSS Oral History Project, September 4, 1996.

68 "Your turn, soldier": Ibid.

68 "After that, everyone called me Sharpshooter": Ibid.

71 "nobody could have saved me": Ibid.

71 "'If you think it will work'": Ibid.

72 "'the Jew in the White House'": Ibid.

73 "where I come from Slovak equals": Ibid.

73 "Say that again, about Roosevelt": Ibid.

73 "He was just too stunned": Ibid.

74 "He would then have to hold": Ibid.

75 "but I was wondering how": Ibid.

76 "They could have spilled the beans": Ibid.

CHAPTER 6: BETTY

79   "Only if they promise to send me": Bergin, "Inside the OSS," July 2007.

79   "I think we can do that": Ibid.

80   "We were taught how to get rumors": McIntosh, OSS Oral History Project, May 2, 1997.

80   "we were changing everything": Elizabeth P. McIntosh and Frederick McIntosh, interview, Elizabeth P. McIntosh Collection [AFC/2001/001/30838], Veterans History Project, American Folklife Center, Library of Congress, November 17, 2002.

81   "We will reproduce the cartoons": Betty MacDonald to Captain Max Kleiman, April 12, 1944, Folder Marigold, Box 424, Entry A1 210, RG 226 OSS/NARA II, US National Archives.

82   "and I would appreciate": Ibid.

83   "I should've picked up the pistol": Miller, *Behind the Lines*, 58.

83   "I didn't know what I was looking at": Laurie Podskalny, "Interview with a World War II Spy" (St. Andrew's Episcopal School, Digital Maryland, 2004), 17, https://collections.digitalmaryland.org/digital /collection/saac/id/3973.

84   "But I got the hang of it": Gene Santoro, "At War with the Enemy's Mind: Conversation with Betty McIntosh," HistoryNet, April 21, 2017, https://www.historynet.com/war-enemys-mind-conversation -betty-mcintosh/.

84   "There were a lot of drinking parties": Miller, *Behind the Lines*, 58.

84   "I felt like a full-blown moron": MacDonald, *Undercover Girl*, 48.

84   "I knew I'd have to write": Ibid., 113–114.

85   "Every paperclip was saved and used again": Ibid., 85–86.

86   "offset makes no physical impression on paper": Ibid., 88.

86   "Japanese newsprint was made": Ibid.

87   "He took one look at us": Bergin, "Inside the OSS," July 2007.

87   "Then, they'd have to treat me": Laurie Podskalny, "Interview with a World War II Spy," 21.

87   "He got demoted for it": Ibid.

87   "We had to crack through the fanatical indoctrination": MacDonald, *Undercover Girl*, 38.

89   "he would do anything to shorten the war": Ibid., 93.

90   "and we had a lot of fun thinking these things up": Bergin, "Inside the OSS," July 2007.

90   "until a suitable male replacement": MacDonald, *Undercover Girl*, 106.

90   "Was this New Year 1945": Ibid., 112.

CHAPTER 7: MARLENE

91   "The public does not want polite drawing room comedies": "Thanks Soldier," Marlene Dietrich Collection Berlin, MarleneDietrich.org.

92   "I need glamour out *here*": Riva, *Marlene Dietrich*, 525.

92   "She really worked with elbow grease": Chandler, *Marlene*, 154–155.

92   "But I figure the boys may enjoy me": "Upcoming Tour of Army Centers," *Binghamton Press and Sun-Bulletin*, February 18, 1944.

93   "Her stomach heaved and she was dizzy": Riva, *Marlene Dietrich*, 535.

94   "guaranteed whistle bait": "USO Camp Shows," *Vogue*, May 1, 1944.

95   "All of our comings and goings": Leo Lerman, "Welcome, Marlene," *Vogue*, August 1944.

95   "We do some skits": Ibid.

97   "When you work for the USO": Ibid.

97   "You never heard such whistling": "Marlene Dietrich Recalls Her D-Day Show at Anzio," *New York Herald Tribune*, June 22, 1944.

98   "who were about to meet up": Riva, *A Woman at War*, 67.

98   "German officials felt she was a traitor": Ibid., 91.

99   "And outdoor shows were never called off": "Marlene All Keyed Up For Berlin Show Next Week," *Brooklyn Daily Eagle*, June 21, 1944.

99   "The authorities had to stop the show": Russel Weiskircher, memoirs edited by Eric Rieth, 45thDivision.org maintained by World War II Recreation Association, last modified January 5, 2020, https://www.45thdivision.org/Veterans/Weiskircher157.htm.

99   "Smelling perfume on a woman": Wieland, *Dietrich & Riefenstahl*, 70.

99   "She lived on cigarettes, coffee and martinis": Weiskircher, memoirs, 45thDivision.org.

100 "That's a marvelous feeling": Lerman, "Welcome, Marlene," August 1944.

100 "That made them the bravest of all": Bach, *Marlene Dietrich*, 295.

100 "I'll go anywhere": "Marlene Dietrich Recalls Her D-Day Show," June 22, 1944.

100 "When she got as close as she could to the border, just to be there and help raise morale, well it impressed him terribly": Riva, *A Woman at War*, 91.

102 "I am German and I understand the Germans": Knopp, *Hitler's Women*, 264.

102 "Even if she had nothing else": Ibid., 308.

CHAPTER 8: JANE

105 "We don't count—we aren't important any more": Jane Smith-Hutton, talk at Fairfield (CT) Library, April 1943.

106 "She added a bit of spit and polish": Elizabeth P. McIntosh, *Sisterhood of Spies: The Women of the OSS* (Annapolis: Naval Institute Press, 1998), 52.

110 "subversive rumors against the enemy": Office of Strategic Services, *Morale Operations Field Manual: Strategic Services Field Manual No. 2* (Washington, DC: Office of Strategic Services, 1943), 16.

110 "whose monotonous, humdrum lives": Ibid., 17.

110 "To cover up the real cause of death": "To Those Concerned," RU-MORS, Folder 1734, Box 130, Entry 139, RG 226 OSS/NARA II, US National Archives.

110 "First they fell into a coma": Ibid.

111 "Most importantly, the rumor should be specific": Ibid.

111 "we have stopped talking about rumors": Ibid.

112 "Nothing remains but tatters": Production Order 1028-A, June 1944, Folder 1734, Box 130, Entry 139, RG 226 OSS/NARA II, US National Archives.

112 "a peace organization of Japanese": Betty MacDonald to Captain Tom Adams, June 2, 1944, "Production," Folder 1734, Box 130, Entry 139, RG 226 OSS/NARA II, US National Archives.

113 "The requested increase in salary is well-deserved": Requested Increase in Salary, Job Description, October 23, 1944, OSS Personnel Files, 1941–1945, Box 726, Entry 224, RG 226 OSS/NARA II, US National Archives.

113 "She is one of the most well-informed": Ibid.

113 "and she is the best available": Letter, Edna F. Stonesifer to Saul Stein, November 20, 1944, OSS Personnel Files, 1941–1945, Box 726, Entry 224, RG 226 OSS/NARA II, US National Archives.

CHAPTER 9: ZUZKA

119 "So, where are you from?": Podoski, OSS Oral History Project, September 4, 1996.

119 "Is it the air raids": Ibid.

120 "She might be screwing another guy": Ibid.

121 "He who rests, rusts": OSS Personnel Files, 1941–1945, Box 436, Entry A1-224, RG 226 OSS/NARA II, US National Archives.

121   "we also want to get pregnant again": Podoski, OSS Oral History Project, September 4, 1996.

122   "Would you care to see the blueprint?": Ibid.

123   "it is a source of embarrassment to her": Memo, May 29, 1944, OSS Personnel Files, 1941–1945, Box 726, Entry 224, RG 226 OSS/NARA II, US National Archives.

123   "She is very highly emotional": Memo, May 18, 1945, OSS Personnel Files, 1941–1945, Box 726, Entry 224, RG 226 OSS/NARA II, US National Archives.

124   "'You're not an officer'": Podoski, OSS Oral History Project, September 4, 1996.

125   "and bitched that my rank": Ibid.

125   "Did you know that the Czechs": Podoski, Women's Memorial Foundation, August 5, 2005.

126   "Only one road leads to the homeland": Amanda Shapiro, *The Propagandist: The Woman Behind WWII's Most Dazzling Intelligence Schemes* (Kindle, 2018), loc. 602.

127   "hence we can never tell": Deirdre Bair, *Saul Steinberg: A Biography* (New York: Nan A. Talese Books, 2012), 127.

128   "whether it had any influence": Cora Du Bois, "Oral History of the Tenured Women in the Faculty of Arts and Sciences at Harvard University, 1981," Session III, Part I, August 20, 1981.

128   "You don't get a body count": Riva, *A Woman at War*, 89.

129   "I wanted desperately to stay in Europe": Podoski, OSS Oral History Project, September 4, 1996.

130   "Loyal, untiring, efficient": Barbara Lauwers, OSS Personnel Files, 1941–1945, Box 726, Entry 224, RG 226 OSS/NARA II, US National Archives.

130   "her leaflets being accountable": Ibid.

CHAPTER 10: MARLENE

132   "I think Marlene made it better": Riva, *A Woman at War*, 91.

134   "There will be a cross on a grave": Marlene Dietrich, *Marlene Dietrich Overseas*, Columbia Records, 1951.

135   "It's you, Lili Marlene": Ibid.

136   "With you, Lili Marlene": Ibid.

137   "many said that they were overcome": Riva, *A Woman at War*, 91.

138   "The long underwear is the only thing": Frank Conniff, "Marlene Dietrich Quits as Film Actress," International News Service, February 2, 1945.

138   "It wasn't easy, but it was wonderful": Riva, *A Woman at War*, 47.

138   "Even when there was an indoors": Ean Wood, *Dietrich: A Biography* (London: Sanctuary, 2002), 225.

139   "She's worked herself to death": Louella O. Parsons, "Carroll Awarded Medal for Red Cross Work," *Rochester Democrat and Chronicle*, December 22, 1944.

139   "Here is this glamorous figure": Riva, *A Woman at War*, 65.

139   "her forehead got so bruised": "Helmets Hurt Marlene As She Kisses G.I.'s," *Glens Falls* (NY) *Post Star*, November 1, 1944.

140   "They'll shave off my hair": Marlene Dietrich, *Marlene* (New York: Grove Press, 1989), 189.

140   "It's small, but it's effective": Ibid., 188.

140   "the old man certainly wouldn't": Ibid.

140   "When the boys think we won't come": "Miss Dietrich Calls G.I.s Most Grateful Public," *New York Herald Tribune*, July 19, 1945.

142   "I hate to see all these ruins": Knopp, *Hitler's Women*, 311.

142   "The owner of the theater": Parsons, "Carroll Awarded Medal for Red Cross Work."

142   "After entertaining troops for a full year": Conniff, "Marlene Dietrich Quits," February 2, 1945.

142   "She rather looked down her nose": Riva, *A Woman at War*, 121.

143   "It made everyone kind of homesick": Ibid., 93.

CHAPTER 11: JANE

145   "The writer who disregards this": Daily Intelligence Summary, February 19, 1944, Folder 2698, Box 123 Entry 92A, RG 226 OSS/NARA II, US National Archives.

146   "and hopes for a democratic and peace-loving": Brian Masaru Hayashi, *Asian American Spies: How Asian Americans Helped Win the Allied Victory* (New York: Oxford University Press, 2021), 107.

147   "TARGET: Japanese Troops": Production Order, August 23, 1944, Folder 1735, Box 130, Entry 139, RG 226 OSS/NARA II, US National Archives.

147   "TARGET: Japanese Women": Ibid.

148   "TOPIC: SENJIN KUN [Battlefield Code]": Production Order, August 23, 1944, Folder 1734, Box 130, Entry 139, RG 226 OSS/NARA II, US National Archives.

149   "even though he may die": Ibid.

150   "our guide is: 'I wish to die'": Ibid.

150   "it is for the upper class at home": Ibid.

150 "we would make R&A happy": Betty MacDonald to Director, Office of Strategic Services, July 28 1944, Folder MO Washington Adm., Box 124, Entry 136, RG 226 OSS/NARA II, US National Archives.

150 "It's believed to be one": Subject: Fake edition of SENJIN KUN, Lieutenant Colonel Herbert S. Little to Carleton Scofield et. al., September 26, 1944, Folder Marigold, Box 424, Entry A1 210, RG 226 OSS/ NARA II, US National Archives.

151 "On the other side, dead soldiers": Major Harley Stevens to Edgar Salinger, April 21, 1944, Folder 1265, Box 122, Entry 136, RG 226 OSS/ NARA II, US National Archives.

151 "Prince Tokugawa, Tojo, and Shimada": Ibid.

153 "No wonder they are screaming": Ann Todd Baum, "Betty and Jane: Two OSS Women Who Waged Psychological Warfare in a Forgotten Theater" (PhD diss., University of Texas at Austin, 2014), 230, http://hdl.handle.net/2152/44077.

153 "what happened to her order": Memo, Captain Bernard White to Elizabeth C. Moore, March 3, 1945, Folder Field Files, Box 122, Entry 136, RG 226 OSS/NARA II, US National Archives.

154 "Hope these #s are what the Coliseum wants": Routing and Record Sheet, April 4, 1945, OSS Personnel Files, 1941–1945, Box 726, Entry 224, RG 226 OSS/NARA II, US National Archives.

154 "under the present promotional policy": William C. McCutcheon Jr. to Captain H. H. Bennett, June 9, 1945, OSS Personnel Files, 1941–1945, Box 726, Entry 224, RG 226 OSS/NARA II, US National Archives.

154 "As these rumors are created": Memo, Subject: Executive Meeting, Major Pacatte to Mrs. Jane Smith-Hutton et al., May 10, 1945, Folder Field Files, Box 122, Entry 136, RG 226 OSS/NARA II, US National Archives.

155 "For security reasons, this should be": Office Memo, Lieutenant Colonel Little to Mr. Smith, July 3, 1945, Folder Field Files, Box 122, Entry 136, RG 226 OSS/NARA II, US National Archives.

CHAPTER 12: BETTY

156 "Look at the pretty bird!": MacDonald, *Undercover Girl*, 129.

157 "Request that as of this date": Subject: Printing Production for MO Branch, John Fistere to Chief, Reproduction Branch, March 1, 1945, Folder Marigold, Box 424, Entry A1 210, RG 226 OSS/NARA II, US National Archives.

158   "You could look way down below": MacDonald, *Undercover Girl*, 149.

158   "I looked at my parachute": Ibid.

158   "Is the owner of Chester here?": Elizabeth P. McIntosh and Frederick McIntosh, interview, Elizabeth P. McIntosh Collection [AFC/2001/001/30838], Veterans History Project, American Folklife Center, Library of Congress, November 17, 2002.

159   "Of course!" Ibid.

159   "For the first time since Pearl Harbor": MacDonald, *Undercover Girl*, 152.

160   "Why die before your time?": Ibid., 178.

161   "And she may also suffer from": Ibid., 177.

162   "a sort of Cinderella nightlife": Ibid., 180.

162   "Betty was queen of the ball": Charles Fenn, *At the Dragon's Gate: With the OSS in the Far East* (Annapolis: Naval Institute Press, 2004), 155.

162   "And we were all very lonely": Jennet Conant, *A Covert Affair: Julia Child and Paul Child in the OSS* (New York: Simon & Schuster, 2011), 185.

162   "The war was hard on a lot": Ibid., 116.

163   "I felt frustrated, brought on by": MacDonald, *Undercover Girl*, 201.

163   "We didn't go out and sleep in the mud": Ibid., 203.

164   "the men in the ranks are": Ibid., 210.

164   "All they seemed to be interested in": Ibid., 209.

165   "and it is going to eradicate": "'Spy Girl' Betty McIntosh," CIA, March 30, 2020, https://www.cia.gov/stories/story/spy-girl-betty-mcintosh/.

166   "The weird truth about MO": McIntosh, OSS Oral History Project, May 2, 1997.

CHAPTER 13: ZUZKA

170   "I helped 'liberate' canned food": Podoski, Women's Memorial Foundation, August 5, 2005.

170   "There was no sign of life": Ibid.

171   "So put a lid on": Ibid.

171   "Mother!": Ibid.

171   "But it was still standing": "She Found America," *Los Angeles Times*, December 9, 1945.

172   "My father came home from camp": Podoski, Women's Memorial Foundation, August 5, 2005.

172   "The problem is now solved": Shapiro, *The Propagandist*, loc. 733.

172   "Last week the Salzburg Festival": "Music: Salzburg, 1945," *Time*, August 27, 1945.

173   "The only opera on this year's program": Ibid.

173   "In fact, there was no one": Podoski, "Me Too," 230.

174   "a souvenir from Salzburg": Podoski, OSS Oral History Project, September 4, 1996.

175   "We can't hire you": Podoski, Women's Memorial Foundation, August 5, 2005.

175   "maybe even execute you": Ibid.

176   "I went to Vienna for a few days": Podoski, "Me Too," 230.

177   "For seven years and nine months": Podoski, Women's Memorial Foundation, August 5, 2005.

177   "the basic equipment every soldier carries": Mila Rechcigl, "In Memoriam: Barbara L. Podoski 1914–2009," Academia.edu.

CHAPTER 14: MARLENE

179   "It was a very difficult time for her": Riva, *A Woman at War*, 133.

179   "Why does it take the nearness of death": "When the Yanks Captured Rome, They Brought Food, Freedom—and Marlene!" *San Francisco Chronicle*, August 13, 1944.

180   "I will never feel that way again": Bach, *Marlene Dietrich*, 363.

180   "She could concentrate on the artistic": Ibid.

181   "The two girls are clever": Harvey Southgate, Records Roundup, *Rochester* (NY) *Democrat and Chronicle*, December 6, 1953.

182   "Only from *you* will they believe it": Riva, *A Woman at War*, 135.

183   "Yet Marlene is always a sellout": Lloyd Shearer, "How to Be Glamorous and Happy at 55," *Parade*, August 2, 1959.

183   "glamour is what I sell": Ibid.

183   "But when I sing my songs": Alexander Walker, "Marlene Dietrich 'Acts Only to Lyrics,'" *Philadelphia Daily News*, June 24, 1967.

183   "I don't have to creep": Jack Richards, "Dietrich Gives Off Magic Even During Talk on Phone," *Vancouver Sun*, September 26, 1964.

183   "It's getting more difficult": Shearer, "How to Be Glamorous and Happy."

184   "How many cheeses": Rex Reed, "But It's All So Boring to Marlene," *Chicago Tribune*, January 12, 1973.

184   "asked me the most stupid questions": Ibid.

184   "She saw it as her duty": Johanna Adorjan, "The Sky Was Green When She Said It," *Der Spiegel*, November 13, 2005.

184   "the most important work I've ever done": Knopp, *Hitler's Women*, 308–9.

184   "The officer's daughter had found": Ibid.

CHAPTER 15: BETTY

185 "this was what people did": MacDonald, *Undercover Girl*, 227.

185 "Up to now there had been purpose": Ibid.

185 "Suddenly, we had no direction": McIntosh, *Sisterhood of Spies*, 236.

185 "And a prize of a promise": MacDonald, *Undercover Girl*, 227.

186 "It was probably the best thing": Ibid., 228.

186 "I had no trouble at all": Podskalny, "Interview with a World War II Spy," 28.

187 "And why did all the girls at home": MacDonald, *Undercover Girl*, 278.

187 "Had the nation even absorbed": Ibid., 291.

188 "which was not a normal way": Conant, *A Covert Affair*, 208.

188 "I was in love and we didn't know": Ibid., 19.

188 "Discussing fashion after all": Santoro, "At War with the Enemy's Mind," April 21, 2017.

189 "Oh, the skullduggery": Peter Edson, "Undercover Girl," Newspaper Enterprise Association, December 1, 1947.

189 "Mrs. MacDonald's account of life": Orville Prescott, "Books of the Times," *New York Times*, November 12, 1947.

189 "I had great difficulty writing": McIntosh, *Sisterhood of Spies*, 1.

190 "A lot of the things we tried": Steven V. Roberts, "In Washington, Even Spies Have Lobbyists," *New York Times*, December 13, 1977.

190 "Never again would I feel so alive": Ann Todd, *OSS Operation Black Mail: One Woman's Covert War Against the Imperial Japanese Army* (Annapolis: Naval Institute Press, 2017), xvii.

CHAPTER 16: JANE

192 "We borrowed cots": Henri Smith-Hutton, *The Reminiscences*, 633.

192 "Paint, brushes, lumber, nails": Ibid., 634.

192 "It was not easy to live in Paris": Ibid.

193 "If ladies approached him": Ibid., 643.

194 "We were glad when we didn't": Ibid., 698–699.

BIBLIOGRAPHY

Alcorn, Robert Hayden. *No Bugles for Spies: Tales of the O.S.S.* New York: David McKay, 1962.

Bach, Steven. *Marlene Dietrich: Life and Legend.* New York: William Morrow, 1992.

Bair, Deirdre. *Saul Steinberg: A Biography.* New York: Nan A. Talese Books, 2012.

Baum, Ann Todd. "Betty and Jane: Two OSS Women Who Waged Psychological Warfare in a Forgotten Theater." PhD diss., University of Texas at Austin, 2014.

Boehm, Edward. *Behind Enemy Lines: WWII Allied/Axis Propaganda.* Secaucus, NJ: Wellfleet Press, 1989.

Breaks, Katherine. "The Ladies of the OSS: The Apron Strings of Intelligence in World War II." Manuscripts and Archives at Yale University, 1991.

Brinkley, David. *Washington Goes to War.* New York: Ballantine Books, 1988.

Brown, Anthony Cave. *The Last Hero: Wild Bill Donovan.* New York: Times Books, 1982.

Chambers, John Whiteclay, II. *OSS Training in the National Parks and Service Abroad in World War II.* Washington, DC: US National Park Service, 2008.

Chandler, Charlotte. *Marlene: Marlene Dietrich, A Personal Biography.* New York: Simon & Schuster, 2011.

Conant, Jennet. *A Covert Affair: Julia Child and Paul Child in the OSS.* New York: Simon & Schuster, 2011.

Delmer, Sefton. *Black Boomerang.* New York: Viking Press, 1962.

Dietrich, Marlene. *Marlene*. New York: Grove Press, 1989.

Du Bois, Cora. "Oral History of the Tenured Women in the Faculty of Arts and Sciences at Harvard University, 1981," Session III, Part I, August 20, 1981.

Fenn, Charles. *At the Dragon's Gate: With the OSS in the Far East*. Annapolis: Naval Institute Press, 2004.

Fitch, Noël Riley. *Appetite for Life: The Biography of Julia Child*. New York: Doubleday, 1997.

Foster, Jane. *An UnAmerican Lady*. London: Sidgwick & Jackson, 1980.

Gable, Michelle. *The Lipstick Bureau*. New York: Graydon House, 2022.

Gueli, Cindy. *Lipstick Brigade: The Untold True Story of Washington's World War II Government Girls*. Washington, DC: Tahoga History Press, 2015.

Hart, Scott. *Washington at War: 1941–1945*. Englewood Cliffs, NJ: Prentice-Hall, 1970.

Hayashi, Brian Masaru. *Asian American Spies: How Asian Americans Helped Win the Allied Victory*. New York: Oxford University Press, 2021.

Heideking, Jurgen, and Christof Mauch, eds. *American Intelligence and the German Resistance to Hitler: A Documentary History*. Oxfordshire, England: Routledge, 1998.

Higham, Charles. *Marlene: The Life of Marlene Dietrich*. New York: Norton, 1977.

Hill, Max. *Exchange Ship*. New York: Farrar & Rinehart, 1942.

Hoke, Henry. *Black Mail*. New York: Reader's Book Service, 1944.

Howe, Ellic. *The Black Game: British Subversive Operations Against the Germans During the Second World War*. London: Queen Anne Press, 1988.

Hymoff, Edward. *The OSS in World War II*. New York: Richardson & Steirman, 1986.

Klingaman, William K. *The Darkest Year: The American Home Front 1941–1942*. New York: St. Martin's Press, 2019.

Knopp, Guido. *Hitler's Women*. New York: Routledge, 2003.

Kushner, Barak. *The Thought War: Japanese Imperial Propaganda*. Honolulu: University of Hawai'i Press, 2006.

Laurie, Clayton D. "Black Games, Subversion, and Dirty Tricks: The OSS Morale Operations Branch in Europe, 1943–1945." *Prologue* 25, no. 3 (Fall 1993), 260.

Laurie, Clayton D. *The Propaganda Warriors: America's Crusade Against Nazi Germany*. Lawrence: University Press of Kansas, 1996.

Lerner, Daniel. *Sykewar: Psychological Warfare Against Germany, D-Day to VE-Day*. New York: G. W. Stewart, 1949.

Lipset, David. *Gregory Bateson: The Legacy of a Scientist*. Boston: Beacon Press, 1982.

MacDonald, Alexander. *Bangkok Editor.* New York: Macmillan, 1949.

MacDonald, Alexander. *My Footloose Newspaper Life.* Bangkok: Post Publishing, 1990.

MacDonald, Elizabeth. *Undercover Girl.* New York: Macmillan, 1947.

Margolin, Leo J. *Paper Bullets: A Brief Story of Psychological Warfare in World War II.* New York: Froben Press, 1946.

Mauch, Christof. *The Shadow War Against Hitler: The Covert Operations of America's Wartime Secret Intelligence Service.* New York: Columbia University Press, 2003.

McIntosh, Elizabeth P. *The Role of Women in Intelligence.* McLean, VA: Association of Former Intelligence Officers, 1989.

McIntosh, Elizabeth P. *Sisterhood of Spies: The Women of the OSS.* Annapolis: Naval Institute Press, 1998.

Miller, Russell. *Behind the Lines: The Oral History of Special Operations in World War II.* New York: St. Martin's Press, 2002.

Morley, Sheridan. *Marlene Dietrich.* New York: McGraw-Hill, 1977.

O'Donnell, Patrick K. *Operatives, Spies, and Saboteurs: The Unknown Story of the Men and Women of WWII's OSS.* New York: Free Press, 2004.

Office of Strategic Services. *Morale Operations Field Manual: Strategic Services Field Manual No. 2.* Washington, DC: Office of Strategic Services, 1943.

Pfeiffer, Jack B. "OSS Propaganda in Europe and the Far East." *Studies in Intelligence,* Fall 1984, 41–56.

Podoski, Barbara. "Me Too." In *On All Fronts: Czechoslovaks in World War II,* edited by Lewis M. White. Boulder, CO: Eastern European Monographs, 1992.

Riva, J. David, ed. *A Woman at War: Marlene Dietrich Remembered.* Detroit: Wayne State University/Painted Turtle, 2006.

Riva, Maria. *Marlene Dietrich.* New York: Alfred A. Knopf, 1993.

Riva, Maria. *Marlene Dietrich: Photographs and Memories.* New York: Alfred A. Knopf, 2001.

Roosevelt, Kermit. Introduction to *War Report of the OSS (Office of Strategic Services).* New York: Walker and Company, 1976.

Russell, Francis. *The Secret War.* New York: Time Life Books, 1998.

Sacquety, Troy J. *The OSS in Burma: Jungle War against the Japanese.* Lawrence: University Press of Kansas, 2013.

Schonberger, Howard. "Dilemmas of Loyalty: Japanese Americans and the Psychological Warfare Campaigns of the Office of Strategic Services, 1943–45." *Amerasia Journal* 16, no. 1 (1990), 21–38.

Seymour, Susan C. *Cora Du Bois: Anthropologist, Diplomat, Agent.* Lincoln: University of Nebraska Press, 2015.

Shapiro, Amanda. *The Propagandist: The Woman Behind WWII's Most Dazzling Intelligence Schemes*. Kindle, 2018.

Smith, Richard Harris. *OSS: The Secret History of America's First Central Intelligence Agency*. Guilford, CT: Lyons Press, 2005.

Smith-Hutton, Henri. *The Reminiscences of Captain Henri Smith-Hutton, US Navy (Retired)*. 2 vols. Naval Institute Oral History. Annapolis: US Naval Institute, 1976.

Soley, Lawrence C. *Radio Warfare: OSS and CIA Subversive Propaganda*. New York: Praeger, 1989.

Spoto, Donald. *Blue Angel: The Life of Marlene Dietrich*. New York: Doubleday, 1992.

Stillwell, Paul, ed. *Air Raid: Pearl Harbor! Recollections of a Day of Infamy*. Annapolis: Naval Institute Press, 1981.

Taylor, Edmond. *Awakening from History*. Boston: Gambit, 1969.

Todd, Ann. *OSS Operation Black Mail: One Woman's Covert War Against the Imperial Japanese Army*. Annapolis: Naval Institute Press, 2017.

Troy, Thomas F., ed. *Wartime Washington: The Secret OSS Journal of James Grafton Rogers 1942–1943*. Frederick, MD: University Publications of America, 1987.

White, Lewis M., ed. *On All Fronts: Czechoslovaks in World War II*. Boulder, CO: Eastern European Monographs, 1992.

Wieland, Karin. *Dietrich & Riefenstahl: Hollywood, Berlin, and a Century in Two Lives*. New York: Liveright, 2015.

Winks, Robin W. *Cloak & Gown: Scholars in the Secret War, 1939–1961*. New York: William Morrow, 1987.

Wood, Ean. *Dietrich: A Biography*. London: Sanctuary, 2002.

INDEX

Allen, Riley, 16
American Broadcasting Station in Europe (ABSIE), 98
American Federation of Musicians, 133
American Fund for Czechoslovak Refugees, 176
American Revolution, 195–196
Andersen, Lale, 137
Arizona National Guard, 36
Arlington National Cemetery, 177, 196
Armed Forces Network, 97
Armstrong, Louis, 91
Army, US, 30
  sexism and, 4, 67, 85, 122–125, 130
  Women's Army Corps in, 33, 63–76, 117–131, 177
Around the World in 80 Days (film), 181
Asama Maru (ship), 45–46
Astaire, Fred, 58
atomic warfare, 155, 166, 191
At the Dragon's Gate (Fenn), 162
Aufricht, Ernst Josef, 56
Austria, 169–170, 172–173, 176

Bacharach, Burt, 182
Bata Enterprises, 26–29
Battle of Britain, 31, 78
Battle of the Bulge, 140
Battle of the Philippine Sea, 82
Belgian Congo (now Democratic Republic of the Congo), 27–28
Benny, Jack, 19

Bergen-Belsen concentration camp, 178
Berno, Harry L., 85
black propaganda. *See* propaganda, black
The Blue Angel (film), 49, 57
Boeing Airplane Company, 83
Boldt, William E., 111
"bomb loneliness" project, 161
Book of the Month club, 189
Brecht, Bertolt, 56, 101
Brno, Czechoslovakia, 24–26, 28–29, 131, 170–172, 175
Bronze Star, 130, 176–177
"The Bugle Call to Charge" (song), 111–112
Burma, 86, 89–90, 150

Calcutta, India, 90, 152–153, 156–157, 158, 186
Campbell, Allen "Hump," 10–14
Cantor, Eddie, 91
Carroll, Jimmy, 132, 135–136, 180
cartoon propaganda, 151–153
Caserta, Italy, 71–73, 117–120, 130
Cedar Rapids Gazette, 42
censorship, wartime, 16, 42, 45, 80–81
Childs, Julia (née McWilliams), 158
China, 34, 40–42, 186
  Allied propaganda operations in, 2, 4, 82, 84–85, 89, 143, 157–166
  literacy rate in, 144–145
  Nanking Massacre in, 149

Choukas, Michael E., 154
CIA, 2
    MacDonald's work with, 190
Civil War, US, 17
Clark, Randall, 109
Clooney, Rosemary, 180–181
Columbia Records, 179
comfort women, 164
Communism, 101, 175, 194
concentration camps, 172, 178, 181–182
Congressional Country Club, Bethesda,
    83
Coolidge, Joseph Randolph, IV, 177
Cooper, Gary, 57
copyright law, US, 133
The Cosmopolitan Marlene Dietrich
    (album), 180–181
Crawford, Joan, 49, 58
Crockett, David C., 125
Cugat, Xavier, 91
Czech embassy, US, 30–33, 65, 68, 176
Czechoslovakia, 24–26, 131
    Communist takeover of, 175
    German occupation of, 27–31, 58,
    125–126, 170–172

Das Neue Deutschland (fake newspaper),
    69–70
Daughters of the American Revolution,
    195–196
Davis, Bette, 92
Daytona Beach, Florida, 33, 63–64
D-Day, 68, 82, 97, 142, 194
DDT, 159, 171
Democrat and Chronicle, 181
Destroyer Squadron 15, US Navy,
    112–113
Destry Rides Again (film), 58
Dewart, William, Jr., 69, 71, 174
Dietrich, Elisabeth, 52, 135–136, 178
Dietrich in Rio (album), 181
Dietrich, Josefine Felsing, 51–54,
    135–136, 178
Dietrich, Louis Otto, 51–53, 136
Dietrich, Marie Magdalene "Marlene"
    acting career of, 49, 55–58, 91, 93,
    137, 142, 179, 181–182
    birth/background of, 51–57
    daughter's birth, 56
    honors/medals awarded to, 179, 184

hospital visits by, 92–93, 99–100
Jewish Relief Fund creation by, 50
languages spoken by, 53
marriage to Sieber by, 56–57, 184
military rank given to, 93, 100
music performance by, 53, 55, 91–95,
    100–102, 132–138, 179–184
MUZAK Project participation by,
    100–102, 132–138, 179–180
Nazi bounty placed on, 4, 132,
    139–140
OSS/MO contributions by, 2–5, 89,
    100–102, 132–138, 179–180, 184,
    190
postwar life of, 178–184
prisoner interrogations by, 141
radio broadcasts by/of, 98, 100–102,
    132–138, 178, 182, 184
sexuality of, 56–57
US citizenship granted to, 51, 58
USO tours by, 93–100, 132, 138–142,
    144, 178, 183–184
war bond campaigning by, 56, 91,
    93–94
"Dietrich Talks on Love and Life" (radio
    show), 182
"Donovan's Dreamers," 5
Donovan, "Wild Bill," 67–68, 163,
    188–189
    propaganda campaigns under, 2–5,
    79, 85, 87, 100–101, 106, 111, 127,
    132, 153
Du Bois, Cora, 127
Dulles, Allen, 190

Edson, Peter, 189
Eisenhower, Dwight, 141
Ellington, Duke, 91
emperor decrees, fake, 87–90

"Falling in Love Again" (song), 57, 181
Fenn, Charles, 162
1st French Paratrooper Regiment, 67
Flowers of Japan (fake magazine),
    151–152
Forgy, Howell M., 21
Fort Lewis, Washington, 37
Fort Meade, Maryland, 93
Fort Oglethorpe, Georgia, 64
45th Infantry Division, 99

Foster, Jane, 153
4th Parachute Division, Germany, 75
France. *See* Paris
French Legion of Honor, 179
Friend (fake magazine), 152

The Garden of Allah (film), 57
Garfield, John, 92
Garland, Judy, 181
German Empire, 36, 53–55
Germany, Nazi, 49, 173
　Czechoslovakia's invasion/occupation
　　by, 27–31, 58, 171–172
　Dietrich bounty placed by, 4, 132,
　　139–140
　"Home to the Reich" program by, 50
　Poland's invasion by, 28
　POWs, 3, 70–76, 117–121, 123–128,
　　130, 141
　propaganda by, 2, 50–51, 80
　propaganda campaigns against, 1–5,
　　68–76, 86, 89, 97–98, 100–102,
　　117–131, 132–138, 143, 144,
　　160–161, 190
　surrender of, 130, 142
Girl Scouts, 189
Glamour, 188
Globe, Arizona, 36–37
Goebbels, Joseph, 50
"Good for Nothin'" (song), 181
the Great Depression, 18, 37–38, 58,
　77, 85
Grew, Alice, 35
Grew, Joseph, 35, 43
Gripsholm (ocean liner), 46–48, 103
Gully, Richard, 139, 142

Hauserová, Božena. *See* Lauwers,
　Barbara "Zuzka"
Hauserová, Karel, Jr., 24–25, 172
Hauserová, Karel, Sr., 24–25, 171–172
Hauserová, Olena, 25
Hauserová, Olga, 24–25, 171–172
Hausherr, Mr. (Swiss minister), 45
Hemingway, Ernest, 102
Hepburn, Katharine, 49, 58
Heppner, Betty. *See* MacDonald,
　Elizabeth Sebree Peet "Betty"
Heppner, Richard, 163, 166, 186,
　188–190

Hess, Alexander, 31
"Hibiscus Blossoms" (MacDonald), 18
Hirohito, Emperor of Japan, 150, 161
　fake decrees by, 87–90
Hiroshima, Japan, 42
　bombing of, 155, 166, 191
Hitler, Adolf, 1, 4, 49–50, 97–98. *See also*
　Germany, Nazi
　assassination attempt on, 70, 73
　suicide of, 130, 142
　toilet paper imprints of, 1, 69, 86
Hollywood Canteen, Los Angeles, 91–92
Hollywood Reporter, 58
the Holocaust, 172, 178, 181–182
Home Front Forecast column, 78
Homer, Joy, 161
"Home to the Reich" program, 50
Honolulu Advertiser, 9, 16–17, 19–21
Honolulu Star-Bulletin, 9, 16–17, 18,
　20–22, 81, 188
Hughes, H. Stuart, 66

ikebana (Japanese flower arranging),
　104–105, 193
India, propaganda campaigns run from,
　4, 84–90, 150, 152–153, 156–157,
　161, 186
issei (native-born Japanese), 88–89, 109,
　144–145
Italy, 68–76, 120–126

Japan
　China's war with, 34, 40–42, 144–145,
　　149
　hostages taken by, 43–48
　Nanking Massacre by, 149
　Pearl Harbor bombing by, 9–17,
　　21–24, 35–36, 42, 44, 51, 59
　POWs, 88–89
　propaganda campaigns against,
　　1–5, 80–81, 86–90, 107–112, 142,
　　144–155, 156–165, 189
　propaganda campaigns by, 145
　Senjin Kun military code manual and,
　　148–150
　surrender of, 166, 191
Japanese internment camps, US,
　145–146
Johnson, Milton, 38
Johnson, Philip, 20

Johnson, Walter, 18
Jub, Winifred, 156
Judgment at Nuremberg (film), 181–182
Junior Guild Reading Project for the
    Blind, 195
J. Walter Thompson agency, 101

Kamikaze Campaign, OSS, 160
Kesselring, Albert, 70
Kismet (film), 93, 137
Kleinstein concentration camp, 172
Knight Without Armour (film), 50
Kolisch, Joseph, 123
Kramer, Stanley, 182
Kunming, China, 82, 84–85, 143,
    157–166, 185–186
Kyser, Kay, 21

Lamarr, Hedy, 92
Lancaster, Burt, 181
Laurel and Hardy, 91
Lauwers, Barbara "Zuzka" (formerly
    Božena Hauserová; later Barbara
    Podoski), 60
  birth/background of, 24–30, 93
  birth of daughter, 174
  career, Army, of, 32–33, 63–76,
    117–131, 177
  careers, civilian, of, 26–27, 28–29, 68,
    169–176, 189
  Coolidge's romance with, 177
  death of, 177
  emigration to US by, 28–29, 172–175
  languages spoken by, 26, 68, 176
  marriage to Lauwers by, 27–28, 33,
    128–129, 173
  marriage to Podoski by, 176
  medals awarded to, 130, 176–177
  OSS/MO work by, 2–5, 64–76, 86, 89,
    97, 111, 113, 117–131, 144, 146,
    154, 160–161, 164, 177, 190
  postwar life of, 169–177, 178, 187,
    189, 191
  prisoner interrogations by, 71–73,
    117–121, 123–126, 128, 146
  as Voice of America writer/
    broadcaster, 174–175, 189
Lauwers, Charles, 27–30, 33, 65,
    128–129
Lauwers, Marina, 174–176

"La Vie en Rose" (song), 181, 184
leaflets, propaganda, 1–2, 4, 69–76, 85,
    86–87, 90, 107, 110–112, 120–122,
    126, 130, 151, 159–161, 163
  inefficiencies in making, 152
  layout's importance in, 144–145
  sample work orders for, 147–148
League of Lonely War Women project,
    OSS, 120–122, 160–161
League of Women Voters, 105
Lenya, Lotte, 101
A Letter From Honolulu column,
    20–22
Library of Congress, 176
Life magazine, 14, 48
"Lili Marlene" (song), 95, 133, 134–138,
    142–143
Literary Guild, 189
Little, Herbert S., 146, 150, 155
Live at the Café de Paris (album), 181
Loesser, Frank, 21

MacArthur, Douglas, 191
MacDonald, Alexander "Alex," 9–11, 15,
    20–22, 162–163
MacDonald, Elizabeth Sebree Peet
    "Betty" (later Betty Heppner; Betty
    McIntosh), 34, 60
  birth/background of, 17–21
  books by, 188–190
  career as journalist/writer, 9–23,
    77–79, 186, 188–190
  China stationing by, 82, 85, 157–166,
    185–186
  CIA work by, 190
  death of, 190
  on Dietrich's war contributions, 98,
    100, 132, 137, 142–143
  India stationing by, 85–90, 156–157
  languages, foreign, spoken by, 9,
    19–21, 79, 88
  marriage to Heppner by, 163, 166,
    186, 188–190
  marriage to MacDonald by, 20–21,
    162–163, 188
  marriage to McIntosh by, 190
  OSS/MO work by, 2–5, 79–90, 93,
    106, 111–113, 127–128, 142–143,
    145, 149–150, 152–153, 156–166,
    173, 177, 185–186, 189, 190

Pearl Harbor bombing and, 9–17, 21–23, 24

postwar life of, 179, 185–190, 191

Magistretti, Bill, 88–89, 156–157

Marlene Dietrich Overseas (album), 180–181

Marlene Sings to Her Homeland (radio show), 98

Martin Roumagnac (film), 179

Marx, Groucho, 19

Masaryk, Jan, 29–30

Masaryk University, 26

May, Mia, 56

McIntosh, Betty. *See* MacDonald, Elizabeth Sebree Peet "Betty"

McIntosh, Frederick Ballard, 190

McWilliams, Julia, 158

Mead, Margaret, 107

"Mean to Me" (song), 132–133

Metzl, Lothar, 101, 133, 135

Miller, Mitch, 179–180

Ming, Jane Ellen Thompson "Ellen," 36–37, 38, 103

Ming, Marcus Aurelius Smith, 36–37, 38

Ming, Mary Louise, 36–37

"Miss Otis Regrets" (song), 132–133, 138

MO. *See* Morale Operations, OSS

Montgomery, Bernard Law, 193

Morale Operations (MO), OSS. *See also* propaganda, black

Dietrich's contributions to, 2–5, 89, 100–102, 132–138, 184, 190

field conditions in, 161–162

Lauwers's work in, 2–5, 64–76, 86, 89, 97, 111, 113, 117–131, 144, 146, 154, 160–161, 164, 177, 190

MacDonald's work in, 2–5, 79–90, 93, 106, 111–113, 127–128, 142–143, 145, 149–150, 152–153, 156–166, 173, 177, 185–186, 189, 190

"MO Blues" in, 127–128

Morale Operations Field Manual for, 110

radio broadcasts by, 2, 4, 90, 97–98, 100–102, 107, 110, 126, 132–138, 145, 159–161, 165, 178

romances/affairs in, 129, 162–163, 173

Smith-Hutton's work in, 2–5, 89, 102, 106–114, 122, 143, 144–155, 164–165, 190

successes and failures, measurement of, 126–128

work process inefficiencies in, 81–82, 152–154, 156–157

Morley, Christopher, 19

Morocco (film), 57

Mozarteum Orchestra, 173

MUZAK Project, OSS, 143

alteration of lyrics in, 133–136

Dietrich's participation in, 100–102, 132–138, 179–180

Nagasaki, Japan, bombing of, 155, 166, 191

Nagel, Laird, 164

Navy, US, 15, 32, 38

Smith-Hutton's service in, 34, 39–48, 103, 112–113, 192–195

Nazis. *See* Germany, Nazi

New Delhi, India, 84–90, 150, 161–162, 186

Newhouse, Norman, 69

New Japan (fake magazine), 152

Newspaper Enterprise Association, 78

newspapers/magazines, as propaganda tools, 1–2, 69, 81, 86, 107–108, 110, 126, 151–153, 160–161

New York City, 29–30, 63, 88, 103, 173–176, 187–190

MUZAK Project in, 100–102, 132–136

Project Marigold operations in, 144–146, 151–153

New Yorker, 69

New York Sun, 69

New York Times, 187, 189

nisei (second-generation Japanese), 88, 109, 145

Normandy invasion. *See* D-Day

Oahuan, 18

Office of Censorship, US, 16

Office of Strategic Services (OSS). *See also* Morale Operations, OSS; propaganda, black

field conditions in, 161–162

field training in, 82–84

Office of Strategic Services (OSS) (cont'd)
radio broadcasts by, 2, 4, 90, 97–98,
100–102, 107, 110, 126, 132–138,
145, 159–161, 165, 178
recruiting for, 79–80
Research & Analysis department of,
65–68, 73, 127, 158, 177
romances/affairs in, 129, 162–163, 173
Secret Intelligence branch of, 64–65
Special Operations branch of, 127, 163
women's employment statistics for,
109
women's job/pay discrimination in,
2–4, 85, 109, 112–114, 122–125,
130, 154, 157
work process inefficiencies in, 81–82,
152–154, 156–157
Office of War Information, US, 155, 169,
173, 174
Officer Candidate School, US Army, 64,
124, 130
Okamoto (Japanese POW), 89
"Oklahoma" (song), 101
Oldfield, Barney, 139
Operation Sauerkraut, 3, 70–76, 130
POW interrogations in, 117–121,
123–126, 128, 146
Oran, Algeria, 65–68
OSS. See Office of Strategic Services

Pacatte, Andre, 154
Palace Under the Sea (Heppner),
189–190
Paramount Pictures, 57, 60
Paris, 139, 183
Dietrich's residence in, 179, 184
Lauwers's residence in, 26
liberation of, 137
Smith-Hutton's residence in, 192–195
Patton, George, 140
Pearl Harbor bombing, 9–14, 16–17, 21,
24, 35–36, 42, 44, 51, 59
casualties/damage in, 15
martial law post-, 15, 22–23
Peet, Frederick, 17
Peet, Frederick Tomlinson, 17
Peet, Jessie Lydia Sebree, 17
Peet, Marjorie, 17
Peet, William, 17
Philippines, 9, 19, 38, 44, 47

photo manipulation, 151
"Physical Training Guide for Industrial
Workers" (propaganda booklet),
151
Podoski, Barbara. See Lauwers, Barbara
"Zuzka"
Podoski, Joseph Junosza, 176
Poland, 28
postcards
alteration of, 4, 69–70, 90
fake, 69–70
Powell, Beverley, 174
POWs. See prisoners of war
"Praise the Lord and Pass the
Ammunition" (song), 21
Prescott, Orville, 189
Presidential Medal of Freedom, 179
prisoners of war (POWs), 4, 88, 110,
127, 141, 186
civilian, 45
embassy, 43–48
international law regarding, 70–72
propaganda campaigns utilizing, 3,
70–76, 89, 117–121, 123–126, 128,
130, 146, 156
Project Marigold, OSS, 144–154
propaganda, black (OSS)
via "bomb loneliness" campaign, 161
via cartoons, 151–153
via comfort women disinformation
campaign, 164
Dietrich's participation in, 2–5, 89,
100–102, 132–138, 184, 190
guilt experienced over, 89–90, 185
via Kamikaze Campaign, 160
Lauwers's creation of, 2–5, 68–76, 86,
89, 97, 111, 113, 117–131, 144, 146,
154, 160–161, 164, 177, 190
via leaflets/pamphlets, 1–2, 4, 69–76, 85,
86–87, 90, 107, 110–112, 120–122,
126, 130, 144–148, 151–152,
159–161, 163
via League of Lonely War Women
campaign, 120–122, 160–161
MacDonald's creation of, 2–5, 80–82,
85–90, 93, 106, 111–113, 127–128,
142–143, 145, 149–150, 152–153,
156–166, 177, 185, 189, 190
via military code manual rewriting,
148–150

via military orders, fake, 2, 70–76, 87–90
via MUZAK Project, 100–102, 132–138, 143, 179–180
via newspaper/magazine stories, 1–2, 69, 81, 86, 107–108, 110, 126, 151–153, 160–161
via Operation Sauerkraut, 3, 70–76, 117–121, 123–126, 128, 130, 146
via photo manipulations, 151
via postcards, altered, 4, 69–70, 90
via postcards, fake, 69–70
POW assistance with, 3, 70–76, 89, 117–121, 123–126, 128, 130, 146, 156
Project Marigold's creation of, 144–154
via radio broadcasts, 2, 4, 90, 97–98, 100–102, 107, 110, 126, 132–138, 145, 159–161, 165, 178
and results, quantification of, 126–128
Rumor Mill sessions for developing, 109–112, 147, 154, 164–165
sample work orders for, 147–148
Smith-Hutton's creation of, 102, 107–114, 143, 144–155, 164–165, 190
via songs, 97–98, 100–102, 111–112, 132–138, 178
susceptibility to, 110
via toilet paper with Hitler imprint, 1, 69, 86
via travel orders to civilians, fake, 156–157
white propaganda vs., 2
work process inefficiencies in, 81–82, 152–154, 156–157
via "yoke of shame" campaign, 126
propaganda, white, 155
black propaganda vs., 2
via radio broadcasts, 98
Purple Heart, 177
Pyle, Ernie, 78

radio
Armed Forces Network, 97
black propaganda, OSS, on, 2, 4, 90, 97–98, 100–102, 107, 110, 126, 132–138, 145, 159–161, 165, 178
black propaganda, Soldatensender West, on, 97, 100
"Dietrich Talks on Love and Life" show on, 182
Marlene Sings to Her Homeland show on, 98
MUZAK Project for, 100–102, 132–138, 143, 179–180
Radio Free Europe, 194
Voice of America, 174–175, 189
white propaganda, ABSIE, on, 98
Radio Free Europe, 194
Red Cross, 19, 85, 99
Research & Analysis division, OSS, 65–68, 73, 127, 158, 177
Richards, Atherton, 79
Riefenstahl, Leni, 50
Riva, Maria Elisabeth Sieber, 50, 93–94, 137, 142, 179, 184
birth of, 56
Rome
Allied forces' capture of, 68
OSS operations in, 68–76, 120–126
Rooney, Mickey, 19
Roosevelt, Eleanor, 77
Roosevelt, Franklin Delano, 42, 51, 59
Rosie and Marlene (album), 180–181
Rumor Mill sessions, OSS, 109–112, 147, 154, 164–165

Salzburg Festival, Austria, 169–170, 172–173
San Francisco Chronicle, 20–22
Schöneberg, Germany, 51–55
Scripps-Howard News Service, 77–78
Secret Intelligence (SI) branch, OSS, 64–65
the Seer (OSS radio announcer), 165–166
"See What the Boys in the Back Room Will Have" (song), 95
Senjin Kun (Japanese military code manual), 148–150
Il Seraglio (opera), 173
sexual favors, 67, 75
Shanghai, 35, 186
Shanghai Express (film), 57
Shearer, Lloyd, 183
"She Watched the Bombing of Honolulu" (MacDonald), 22

Shimada, (Japanese admiral), 151
Shore, Dinah, 91
Sieber, Maria. *See* Riva, Maria Elisabeth
    Sieber
Sieber, Rudolf, 56–58
Sioux City Journal, 39
Smith-Hutton, Cynthia, 34–35, 39–40,
    43, 103, 192
    birth of, 38
Smith-Hutton, Henri, 34, 39–48, 103,
    106, 112–113, 192–195
    death of, 196
Smith-Hutton, Jane Ming, 51, 60, 93
    birth/background of, 34, 36–40
    birth of daughters, 38, 191
    China/Japan residence by, 40–46
    death of, 196
    as Japanese hostage, 43–48
    languages spoken by, 34, 41, 106–107
    marriage to Johnson by, 38
    OSS/MO work by, 2–5, 89, 102,
        106–114, 122, 143, 144–155,
        164–165, 190
    Paris relocation by, 192–195
    Pearl Harbor attack and, 35–36
    postwar life of, 191–196
    Project Marigold participation by,
        144–154
    Rumor Mill sessions by, 109–112,
        147, 154, 164–165
    Smith-Hutton's marriage to, 39–40
    volunteer work by, 194–196
Smith-Hutton, Marcia, 192, 195
    birth of, 191
Social Register, 79
Soldatensender West (radio station),
    97, 100
songs, as propaganda tools, 97–98,
    100–102, 111–112, 132–138, 178
"The Song of a Young Sentry" (poem), 134
Southgate, Harvey, 181
Spanish Flu, 55
Special Operations, OSS, 127, 163
Speicher, Steve, 195
SS *President Hoover,* 40
Stadium High School, Tacoma, 37–38
Steinberg, Saul, 69, 127, 174
Stewart, James, 58
Stonesifer, Edna F., 113
Surrender of Caserta, WWII, 130

Tacoma, Washington, 37–38
"Taking a Chance on Love" (song),
    133–134
Theresienstadt labor camp, 171–172
"This Can't Be Love" (song), 101
Thomas, Danny, 93
Thompson, H. O., 42
310 Czechoslovak Fighter
    Squadron, 31
The Threepenny Opera, 56, 101
Time magazine, 172
"Time on My Hands" (song), 132–133,
    138
toilet paper, propaganda on, 1, 69, 86
Tojo, Hideki, 151
Tokugawa (prince of Japan), 151
Tokyo, 191–192
    US embassy in, 34–36, 41–45
"Too Old to Cut the Mustard" (song),
    180–181
Tracy, Spencer, 181–182
Tragedy of Love (film), 56
Tsingtao, China, 40–41
Turner, Lana, 91
2677th Regiment, US, 67, 125, 127

UCLA, 38
Uncle Vanya (play), 19
Undercover Girl (MacDonald),
    188–189
University of Hawaii, 19
University of Iowa, 38
University of Oregon, 37
University of Paris, 26
University of the Philippines, 38
University of Washington, 19,
    189
US embassy, Tokyo, 34–36, 41–45
USO tours, 93–94, 97–100, 132, 142,
    183–184
    conditions on, 95–96, 138–141, 178
USS *Augusta,* 40
USS *Lawrence,* 39
USS *Little Rock,* 191
USS *Missouri,* 191

Variety, 60
Vienna Boys Choir, 169
Vietnam, 47
    War, 195

Voice of America, 174–175, 189
von Losch, Eduard, 53–54, 136

war bonds, 5, 59, 91, 93–94, 105
Waseda University, Tokyo, 88
Washington Daily, 19
Washington, DC, 17, 30–33, 78, 176,
    187–188
  growth of, 77, 103–104
  OSS operations in, 2, 64–65, 79–84,
    106–114, 146, 152–153,
    189–190
Washington Herald, 17
Washington Post, 122
Watanabe, Keiko, 20
Watanabe, Saburo, 20
Weill, Kurt, 101
Weiskircher, Russ, 99
Welles, Orson, 95, 183
We Were in the Battle of Britain (Hess),
    32
Where the Blue Begins (play), 19
white propaganda. *See* propaganda,
    white
Wilder, Billy, 50, 181

Wilhelm II, (king of Prussia), 53
women, labor discrimination against,
    2–4, 9, 16, 20, 33, 67–68, 77, 85,
    109, 112–114, 122–125, 130, 154,
    157, 175–176, 186–187
World War I (WWI), 10, 36, 134
  Dietrich and, 53–55
World War II (WWII)
  atomic warfare of, 166
  Battle of Britain in, 31, 78
  Battle of the Bulge in, 140
  Battle of the Philippine Sea in, 82
  comfort women of, 164
  Czechoslovakia's invasion preceding,
    27–31, 58, 171–172
  D-Day in, 68, 82, 97, 142, 194
  Pearl Harbor bombing in, 9–17,
    21–24, 35–36, 42, 44, 51, 59
  Poland's invasion in, 28
  Surrender of Caserta in, 130
  surrender of Germany in, 130, 142
  surrender of Japan in, 166, 191

"yoke of shame" propaganda campaign,
    126

ABOUT THE AUTHOR

Sharona Jacobs

Lisa Rogak is the bestselling author of numerous books, including *And Nothing But the Truthiness: The Rise (and Further Rise) of Stephen Colbert* and *Angry Optimist: The Life and Times of Jon Stewart*. She is the editor of the *New York Times* bestseller *Barack Obama in His Own Words*. Rogak lives in New Hampshire. Learn more at www.lisarogak.com.